Ready?: Evangelism for Everyo
best book on evangelism I've r
warming, guilt-removing and v

Marcus Honeysett
Director, Living Leadership; Author, *Powerful Leaders:*
When Christian Leadership Goes Wrong and How to Prevent It

This is the book for which I have long been waiting. Informative, inspirational and, at times, provocative. Quick fixes are exposed, and longstanding yet unquestioned evangelistic practices are winsomely critiqued.

David Meredith
Mission Director, Free Church of Scotland, Inverness

Andy Paterson's book *Ready? Evangelism for Everyone* is just what you need to, well, be ready to share the good news. But, it's not just for you. It's an accessible resource for you and your entire church. This book is a gift that will keep on giving, helping people to share the good news of the gospel to a world in need of God's grace.

Ed Stetzer
Dean, Talbot School of Theology, Biola University,
La Mirada, California

Ready?

Evangelism for Everyone

Andy Paterson

CHRISTIAN
FOCUS

Scripture quotations taken from the Holy Bible, New International Version. Copyright © 1973, 1978, 1984 by International Bible Society except where ESV is indicated in the text. Used by permission of Hodder & Stoughton Publishers, A member of the Hodder Headline Group. All rights reserved. 'NIV' is a registered trademark of International Bible Society. UK trademark number 1448790.

Copyright © Andy Paterson 2024

paperback ISBN 978-1-5271-1095-3
ebook ISBN 978-1-5271-1123-3

Published in 2024 by
Christian Focus Publications Ltd,
Geanies House, Fearn, Ross-shire,
IV20 1TW, Great Britain.
www.christianfocus.com

Cover design by James Amour

Printed and bound by Bell and Bain, Glasgow

Contents

To Bev Savage,

So grateful for three special and formative years working as
Assistant to this godly and visionary pastor.

Preface

Many years ago, whilst preparing a preaching series on Colossians, I stumbled across comments by Dick Lucas in his BST commentary on that letter. It was the first time I had ever come across the distinction between direct and responsive evangelism in regard to chapter 4 verse 6. Suddenly, things began to fall into place. It made sense. It resonated. And this little book is a simple attempt to unpack those implications more fully.

I am not proposing something new. My heart's desire is to see every follower of Jesus Christ show and share this wonderful saving grace with all those they interact with. This cannot be reduced to simple formulae or the latest programme or fad. This is about heart and head working together with delight and joy in Christ. Guilt-free and passion-driven!

I want to thank all my colleagues at the FIEC for their partnership over this last decade and for their encouragement to get this published as I step back as Mission Director. It has been an incredible privilege to serve the FIEC family of churches and a joy to witness its ongoing growth and expansion. For the last four years this joy has been doubled through sharing ministry responsibilities between the FIEC and Charlotte Chapel in Edinburgh where a remarkable team encourage and stimulate each other to serve the Lord to the best of their abilities. I am grateful to each one.

As the bibliography will testify, I've tried to engage with many books on evangelism over the years and although there will be areas of significant divergence with some, my love and admiration for all those who long to share the good news of Jesus Christ with others is unbounded and genuine.

I've been grateful for all input into this project, especially from Dr Steve Wilmshurst, an old colleague from Bristol days. And, of course, I owe so much to the love, patience and encouragement of my best friend and wonderful wife, Kath.

Andy Paterson,
Edinburgh
June 2022

Chapter One

Guilty

Clammy skin. Racing pulse. Afraid they might have heard us. The sound of approaching footsteps. Panic as a light goes on and the door swings open. Then hearing my voice. 'Good evening. We're from the local church and we've come to talk to you about Jesus'.

Sometimes they swore, sometimes the door was slammed in our faces, sometimes there was an attempt at intellectual argument, but, worst of all, most of the time they were ... nice. Perhaps patronising (after all we were just a couple of fifteen-year-old lads), but mostly polite in their dismissal of us. And this went on month after month, each time having steeled ourselves for the effort, feeling guilty if we couldn't make the visits.

We knew it was the right thing to do. We knew that without coming to a saving faith in Jesus Christ men and women would be eternally lost. We knew they lived in ignorance of the greatest good news that the whole universe had ever known. We had to let them know. We had to share what had happened to us. But we did so with little joy and a whole lot of unease and discomfort. It just seemed so forced, so unnatural. And we felt guilty.

No doubt my own experience will resonate with some reading this book. We know evangelism is a 'good thing'; it's just the way we go about it can seem strangely disconnected from the world we live in. I've travelled on the London Underground and heard mini sermons shouted out to captive tube passengers between stops. Is that what I should be doing? Is that what evangelism is all about? I've heard Bible verses fired out through mini PA systems to crowds thronging into a Springsteen concert. I've walked through a busy shopping centre and been harangued by a preacher with a bullhorn. I've witnessed tracts being systematically slipped into books at the local library. And all the time my sense of failure as a believer grows because I know I just couldn't do what they're doing. It would seem so personally unnatural.

And what makes it worse is that there are Christians who just love to do this stuff. You can't stop them. They seem energised whenever they get the opportunity to witness, whether that be door-to-door, street work, sketch board or market stall. If they sit next to someone on the train or plane they invariably strike up a conversation that points to Christ, whilst I would sit there hoping for some peace and quiet! That's then compounded by *them* telling *me* that I should be doing what they're doing, that evangelism embraces a *Star Trek* philosophy of outreach – boldly going where no one has gone before.

The truth is I have massive respect and admiration for their drive and passion, and often have tried to copy their techniques and programmes. However, the reality is that these resolutions of mine fade away within a few weeks of rejections and disappointment, and once again the dark cloud of guilt descends upon this rubbish believer who wants to make Christ known but finds the methodologies of others so alien.

Perhaps this explains why so few Christians today seem engaged in sharing their faith, why so many find it easier to hide away in a Christian ghetto, why it is easier to keep your head down than speak up for Jesus. This is compounded by the apparent failure of many gospel people to unpack God's Word. Preachers, who for the most part would carefully exposit sections of the Bible, seem either to be silent on the whole subject of evangelism or else flip-flop into pragmatic suggestions reminiscent of twenty-first century marketing programmes. More than that, when it comes to 'church' theological insight disappears when confronted by 'evangelism'. Rather than being a gathered community of believers, church morphs into a building-centred entity, from which 'outreach' takes place in the hope of capturing a few more who will attend the same building we do.

So, what's happened to evangelism? Is this how it is meant to be? Indeed, is this how it has always been? The intention of this book is to revisit what the Bible teaches with an expectation that we will gain a new vision of what it really means to share the wonderful saving news of Jesus Christ. We'll discover that every single follower of Jesus Christ has a role to play in ways that are both natural and free from false guilt. Of course, it may also challenge the sinful laziness of our hearts and expose the fig-leaf lies that we use to cover over our feeble excuses. And that will be no bad thing when the eternal destiny of the lost is at stake and the honour and glory of Christ is to the fore.

Chapter Two

Tell me the old, old story

I'm indebted to the Gideons. They'd invited me to speak at their national gathering in Birmingham and had gently suggested I might like to consider speaking on their 'theme' verse from 1 Chronicles 16:24: 'Declare his glory among the nations'. Now to my shame I have to confess that I'd never really engaged with that verse before, but the speaking opportunity forced me to drill down into this unexpected diamond-mine. And what I discovered was that 'evangelism' had always been part of God's plan for his people, even during the formation and shaping of the nation of Israel.

This particular verse from Chronicles was a direct quote from words already used in the nation's hymn-book (Ps. 96:3). It tells us something of what we should be declaring, how we should declare it, and where that is to be made known.

So – what was it that God's people were to declare?

The answer is – 'his glory'. But this is where our problem lies. What on earth does that mean? It seems to be one of those Bible expressions that we grow up with but can rarely define. It feels like something big and shiny, but as soon as we try to put it into words it begins to feel like nailing jelly to a wall.

For some of us, glory is what we associate with events in the past: when things went well, when there were particular times of triumph and achievement. We called them the glory days;

days of lost innocence, days of inexhaustible energy, days of long, hot, uncomplicated summers. And no doubt your mind travels back to such times.

My own experience of glory was being brought up in north-east London and being taken to see the double-winning Spurs side in 1961 as a five-year-old. That was glory. And when you went to White Hart Lane, ringing the hoardings was Spur's motto – 'The game is about glory'.

But is this what the Bible writers mean? And when we look more closely, we discover that they use that word 'glory' in one of two ways.

Firstly, it's used in the sense of describing what God is like – what theologians call the attributes of God – his beauty and splendour, his holiness and power, his supremacy and rule, his majesty and compassion.

The following verses give some idea of how 'glory' is used in this way:

> Yours, LORD, is the greatness and the power and the ***glory*** and the majesty and the splendour, for everything in heaven and earth is yours. Yours, LORD, is the kingdom; you are exalted as head over all (1 Chron. 29:11).

> LORD, our Lord, how majestic is your name in all the earth! You have set your ***glory*** in the heavens (Ps. 8:1).

> The heavens declare the ***glory*** of God; the skies proclaim the work of his hands (Ps. 19:1).

> for all have sinned and fall short of the ***glory*** of God (Rom. 3:23).

And in the Old Testament this Hebrew word for glory – *kavode* – occurs 144 times, whilst the equivalent Greek word – *doxa* – appears 115 times in the NT.

But this word for glory is predominantly used in another way. Not to describe God's awesome character in general, but specifically to refer to his character being revealed physically to sinful people. And so, when you get references to light and fire and cloud, it is often summarised by the word 'glory'.

Let me give you some illustrations of what I mean.

While Aaron was speaking to the whole Israelite community, they looked toward the desert, and there was the *glory* of the LORD appearing in the cloud (Exod. 16:10).

and the *glory* of the LORD settled on Mount Sinai. For six days the cloud covered the mountain, and on the seventh day the LORD called to Moses from within the cloud (Exod. 24:16).

To the Israelites the *glory* of the LORD looked like a consuming fire on top of the mountain (Exod. 24:17).

Then the cloud covered the tent of meeting, and the *glory* of the LORD filled the tabernacle. Moses could not enter the tent of meeting because the cloud had settled on it, and the *glory* of the LORD filled the tabernacle (Exod. 40:34-35).

Then the LORD will create over all of Mount Zion and over those who assemble there a cloud of smoke by day and a glow of flaming fire by night; over everything the *glory* will be a canopy (Isa. 4:5).

You've maybe heard this referred to as the Shekinah glory, a phrase used later by the rabbis to describe the presence of God in the pillar of cloud and fire. You'll maybe remember how the glory of God appeared to lead the people across the sea and through the wilderness and how, at Sinai, with Israel encamped around the mountain, the glory of God comes in the cloud and fire to speak with Moses in the sight of the people.

This picture of Israel encamped around the glory of God on Sinai portrays God dwelling in the midst of his people. Later, the same glory filled the new temple that Solomon builds. God was in their midst.

So, do you get it? The glory of God is often a reference to the amazing miracle that the infinitely glorious and holy and powerful God comes to dwell with his people in all their sin and failure. Now this really is glorious. This is astounding. And this is the way the word 'glory' is used in Psalm 96.

It's in this sense rather than the more general definition of glory, that we're to understand what it is that the Israelites were to declare. And we know that because of the lines that surround the words 'declare his glory' in Psalm 96 verse 3.

Have another look at them:

Sing to the LORD, praise his name;
proclaim his salvation day after day.
Declare his glory among the nations,
his marvellous deeds among all peoples.

This is Hebrew poetry. And Hebrew poetry operates according to 'parallelism' in which surrounding lines repeat, develop or explain what the poet wants to say.

And what do the surrounding lines to 'Declare his glory' say? What's another way of understanding this phrase better?

'proclaim his salvation', 'declare … his marvellous deeds'.

So the glory to be declared isn't something vague and general. We've got to go beyond big clichés, however wonderful they may be, to declare that our God, in all his infinite glory and wonder and splendour, is best seen and known through the fact that he pleases to make himself known to, and dwell with, sinful people. That's 'glory'.

And this is where it gets even more exciting. That word for salvation ('proclaim his salvation') gives us a clue as to where God's saving glory is most clearly seen, where it finds its perfect embodiment. In Hebrew that word for salvation is 'Yeshua'. Now does that ring any bells? Of course it does. This is where the name 'Jesus' comes from.

'An angel of the Lord appeared to him in a dream and said, "Joseph son of David, do not be afraid to take Mary home as your wife, because what is conceived in her is from the Holy Spirit. She will give birth to a son, and you are to give him the name Jesus, because he will save his people from their sins"' (Matt. 1:20-21).

Jesus – Joshua – 'the Lord saves'. And in John's summary verse of the birth of Jesus he says this:

> The Word became flesh and made his dwelling among us. We have seen his glory, the glory of the one and only Son, who came from the Father, full of grace and truth (John 1:14).

And when John says that Jesus 'made his dwelling among us' it could more literally be translated as Jesus 'tabernacled' among us and 'we have seen his glory'.

John deliberately likens the coming of Jesus to the Shekinah glory. Just as the glory of God was evident when the tabernacle was erected in the centre of the Israelite camp, so Jesus is the perfect representation of God among sinful people. It is in Jesus that we see the glory of God.

And Luke gets in on this as well. He wants us to see the connection. Listen to the words of Simeon when he holds baby Jesus in the temple:

> Sovereign Lord, as you have promised, you may now dismiss your servant in peace. For my eyes have seen your salvation, which you have prepared in the sight of all nations: a light for revelation to the Gentiles, and the glory of your people Israel (Luke 2:29-32).

Jesus – the light of God's glory, the perfect embodiment of God's glorious character, the complete sum of all God's majestic attributes, the Saviour of sinners.

We see this pictured again when Jesus was transfigured before three of his disciples. Listen to Matthew's account and get a glimpse of what he's describing:

> After six days Jesus took with him Peter, James and John the brother of James, and led them up a high mountain by themselves. There he was transfigured before them. His face shone like the sun, and his clothes became as white as the light. Just then there appeared before them Moses and Elijah, talking with Jesus (Matt. 17:1-3).

Do you notice Matthew doesn't name the mountain they went up? It was probably Tabor or Hermon, but that's not his point. He's drawing another parallel. He wants this 'high mountain' to resonate with his Jewish readers so they think of Sinai, of fire, of Moses, of glory. For Jesus is the Shekinah glory. He is God's salvation.

And when God's people, by his wonderful saving grace, end up in heaven, we'll live in the light of his glory. God will dwell among his people. We'll see Jesus. We'll serve in the light of his Shekinah glory.

> No longer will there be any curse. The throne of God and of the Lamb will be in the city, and his servants will serve him. They will see his face, and his name will be on their foreheads. There will be no more night. They will not need the light of a lamp or the light of the sun, for the Lord God will give them light. And they will reign for ever and ever (Rev. 22:3-5).

So, you see what it was that God's people were expected to declare – 'his glory', who we can now name as Jesus. He's the one we're to declare, he's the one we're to point to, he's the one who must be the centre of all our energies, he's the one who must fuel our passion.

But how were God's people to declare this glorious Jesus?

The Hebrew word used here for 'Declare' is *'caphar'*. It's used 109 times in the OT, and on 33 occasions it has the sense of numbering or counting. For example:

> He [the Lord] took him [Abram] outside and said, "Look up at the sky and count the stars—if indeed you can count them". Then he said to him, "So shall your offspring be" (Gen. 15:5).

> Walk about Zion, go around her, count her towers, consider well her ramparts, view her citadels, that you may tell of them to the next generation (Ps. 48:12-13).

And the sense here is that the psalmist was encouraging the worshippers to be strengthened by a knowledge of what God had done for Jerusalem.

This numbering or counting or reckoning is all to do with a sense of amazement at what God had done. And before God's people could ever 'declare his glory among the nations' they needed to have seen and experienced the wonder of his salvation. There needed to be the 'wow' factor.

This is exactly what Isaac Watts was getting at.

> When I survey the wondrous cross
> On which the Prince of glory died,
> My richest gain I count but loss,
> And pour contempt on all my pride.

> Forbid it, Lord, that I should boast,
> Save in the death of Christ my God!
> All the vain things that charm me most,
> I sacrifice them to His blood.

> See from His head, His hands, His feet,
> Sorrow and love flow mingled down!
> Did e'er such love and sorrow meet,
> Or thorns compose so rich a crown?

> Were the whole realm of nature mine,

That were a present far too small;
Love so amazing, so divine,
Demands my soul, my life, my all.

Before ever I can declare the glory of Jesus, I need to have seen and felt and tasted and experienced the wonder of what he's done. I need a new view of my sin, of how it permeates my every faculty all the time, how it's an infinite offence to an infinitely holy God, how without Christ I'm justly and eternally lost and separated from the Creator, how his burning wrath bore down upon my soul.

But then there is a second way the Hebrew word for 'declare' is used in the Old Testament. It has the sense of telling another what you've seen or experienced for yourself. Perhaps the word 'recount' expresses this sense best. Let me give you some examples of the way the word is used and you'll see what I mean.

> Moses **told** his father-in-law about everything the LORD had done to Pharaoh and the Egyptians for Israel's sake and about all the hardships they had met along the way and how the LORD had saved them (Exod. 18:8).

> 'Pardon me, my lord,' Gideon replied, 'but if the LORD is with us, why has all this happened to us? Where are all his wonders that our ancestors **told** us about …?' (Judg. 6:13).

> The king was talking to Gehazi, the servant of the man of God, and had said, "**Tell** me about all the great things Elisha has done" (2 Kings 8:4).

In Job 15 verse 17 Eliphaz says 'Listen to me and I will explain to you; let me **tell** you what I have seen'.

And probably the best place we can see this all coming together is in Psalm 48:12-13 where the word is used twice in slightly different ways.

'Walk about Zion, go around her, count [reckon] her towers, consider well her ramparts, view her citadels, that you may tell [recount] of them to the next generation'.

So, if God's people were to 'declare his glory among the nations', it means they not only had to be those who'd seen and experienced that glory for themselves, it also means they were to go on and share that wonderful news with others. And that's certainly the main sense of what's being said in the Psalm – 'tell others about the wonders of his salvation that you've come to know for yourself'.

The final sense of this Hebrew word '*caphar*' means 'to write down, to make a written record'.

> … if you obey the LORD your God and keep his commands and decrees that are **written** in this Book of the Law (Deut. 30:10).

> This is what the LORD, the God of Israel, says: '**Write** in a book all the words I have spoken to you (Jer. 30:2).

So, part of declaring the glory of God – the wonder of his salvation in Christ – is that it will be written down and distributed among the nations. (You can see why this verse was such an appropriate one for the Gideon movement, with their passion to distribute Bibles everywhere.)

One of the most interesting gospel developments I've noticed over the last five years is how studying the Bible with another person is proving to be the most effective evangelistic tool we know. We've had great courses, like Christianity Explored and Alpha, but their creators recognise that nothing beats sharing God's Word one-to-one. It has its own power and authority, and the wonderfully God-breathed Word reveals Christ with brilliance and authenticity.

The final question is where were God's people to declare his saving glory?

The simple and straightforward answer is 'among the nations', but that would fail to communicate the impact that verse had upon the original readers of the chronicler's account.

It would appear that the chronicler worked sometime around 450–400 BC. Now we're not sure who the chronicler was. Some suggest it could have been Ezra the scribe although most scholars now suggest it may have been another priest or Levite who was working in the temple around that time. But what we do know for sure is that the primary audience for this book was that small rag-tag bunch of exiles who had returned to Israel from Babylon. Remember most stayed behind and didn't make the journey. There was little enthusiasm for two to three generations of Israelites to leave the homes they had comfortably established in Babylonia.

So just for one moment put yourself in the place of those first listeners. Imagine what life was like for them. Picture the thoughts that ran through their minds.

They'd probably returned to Israel full of hope and expectation. Jeremiah had spoken about a new covenant and a new king. Haggai and Zechariah had prophesied that God would overthrow kingdoms and that once again Jerusalem would be the economic, political and spiritual centre of the world. This was exciting. It seemed a bright future lay ahead.

But their hopes were soon shattered. The political superpowers of Persia and Greece dominated the scene. Palestine was just an insignificant cultural backwater, politically impotent. Other religions loomed large, including the Samaritans with their temple on Mount Gerizim, the Persians with their great cult religions, and the Greeks with their mystery religions and stories of the gods who lived on top of Mount Olympus.

As for the Jews, all they had to show for it was the temple they'd just built, and that didn't compare with the magnificent building that Solomon had erected centuries before. And they didn't even have the Ark of the Covenant any longer. It had been lost or destroyed and isn't mentioned again. So sad. So depressing. Just give up hope and keep your head down.

Nothing of the sort! Just notice how the chronicler encouraged his readers.

He looked back to the 'good old' days when David was king, Israel was dominant and temple worship was glorious, and in effect says this – 'It might not look or feel like that now, but what was true then is still true today. And, therefore, we'll make his truth known to all the people who live so proudly around us – Declare his glory among the nations, his marvellous deeds among all people'.

God rules absolutely. And he does so now. These are great times to be alive and serving him. What a privilege to be in a land where God has allowed sin to show its hand, so that the wonder of Christ might be seen all the more clearly. What a privilege to be people of hope and confidence in an age of confusion and despair. What a joy to be safe in the arms of our loving God.

For God's intention was never to limit this salvation to just one people group. He did indeed raise up the Jews to make his character and ways known but his salvation was never to be confined to them.

Listen to God's great covenant promise to Abram:

I will make you into a great nation, and I will bless you;
I will make your name great, and you will be a blessing.
I will bless those who bless you, and whoever curses you
I will curse; and all peoples on earth will be blessed
through you (Gen. 12:2-3).

And the psalmist certainly understood this. Just listen to the references we find in Psalm 96.

Sing to the LORD, all the earth … Declare his glory among the nations, his marvellous deeds among all peoples. … Ascribe to the LORD, all you families of nations, ascribe to the LORD glory and strength ... tremble before him, all the earth. Say among the nations, "The LORD reigns".

And that message continues to circle the globe. And even though so much of the face of this planet has been covered by the Christian message, the task still remains great. As I write, of the 16,464 people groups in our world, 6,659 have still to be reached. Of the 7.29 billion people on earth, 3.06 billion live within these unreached people groups.

And God's great purpose is to save representatives from every one of these groups.

The wonder of heaven is that we'll find ourselves standing with them.

> And they sang a new song, saying: "You are worthy to take the scroll and to open its seals, because you were slain, and with your blood you purchased for God persons from every tribe and language and people and nation. You have made them to be a kingdom and priests to serve our God, and they will reign on the earth" (Rev. 5:9-10).

> After this I looked, and there before me was a great multitude that no one could count, from every nation, tribe, people and language, standing before the throne and before the Lamb. They were wearing white robes and were holding palm branches in their hands. And they cried out in a loud voice: "Salvation belongs to our God, who sits on the throne, and to the Lamb" (Rev. 7:9-10).

So, this 'evangelism' we're talking about in this book is no new invention. It's what God's people have been doing all the time. We're just trying to work out how we fit into this continuing story.

Chapter Three

We're all evangelists now ... aren't we?

Bruce Larson, talking of his experience in leadership at University Presbyterian Church of Seattle, said this: 'I proposed to the Session, "How about dropping the evangelism department? Every member of this church is called to be an evangelist, to talk about Jesus to the people where we live and work. Having a department responsible for this lets us off the hook. Let's make evangelism everybody's job". That challenge needed some explaining, of course. We had to help our congregation understand that evangelists aren't scholars who teach theology, though occasionally they are. An evangelist is an introducer. Not everyone can teach; anybody can introduce. An evangelist merely says to someone experiencing the pain of life, "Have you had enough? I want you to meet the ultimate Someone who can change your life—Jesus Christ"'.[1]

But are we all evangelists? We're certainly all called to evangelise, but this is where the confusion arises. By failing to recognise that 'evangelist' is a specialist people gift given to the church by Christ we can make two significant mistakes. Firstly, if we assume that we're all evangelists, then those who are will expect us to evangelise in just the same way they do. They don't see that their gifting is unique to evangelists, and by laying the burden upon 'non-evangelists' to be 'evangelists' they can so easily discourage to the extent that many will give up on evangelism all together. They just can't do it, and that was never the intention of the evangelist, just the sad outcome. Secondly, if we assume that every believer is an evangelist it inevitably flattens out our understanding of the gift. We fail to appreciate the unique character and particular gifting of those who are Christ-called evangelists. And just as in Bruce Larson's church, evangelists will no longer be identified, set apart, trained, resourced and prayed for. How many churches do you know where they have developed the role of the evangelist? We're far more likely to see full time administrators and youth workers on staff than we are to see evangelists. And that imbalance is all down to a failure to engage with the Bible as we ought.

So having made such an accusation, I want to demonstrate what I think emerges from the Scriptures. This might be the time your eyes begin to glaze over and you hurry on to chapter summaries, but get some caffeine in you and let's work this through.

The noun 'evangelist' comes from the Greek verb *euangelizomai* 'to announce news'. And that verb occurs fifty-five times in the New Testament.

The noun itself ('evangelist') occurs only three times. It's used to describe Philip (Acts 21:8), to encourage Timothy (2 Tim. 4:5) and to recognise that 'evangelist' is a people gift to the church (Eph. 4:11). It would be worth stopping off at that passage in Ephesians to notice something very obvious.

'So Christ himself gave the apostles, the prophets, the evangelists, the pastors and teachers, to equip his people for works of service, so that the body of Christ may be built up until we all reach unity in the faith and in the knowledge of the Son of God and become mature, attaining to the whole measure of the fullness of Christ' (Eph. 4:11-13).[2]

Are we all apostles? No. Are we all prophets? No. Are we all pastors and teachers? No.

So ... are we all evangelists? The answer is clearly – no. Evangelist is a people gift from Christ to the church that we should treasure, recognise and cultivate. God give us more evangelists!

But that begs another question – what do evangelists do? What gifts, qualities and characteristics mark them out?

Now to answer that I want to suggest that the apostles, by definition and calling, were equipped and empowered to do the work of an evangelist, and by looking at how they operated in communicating the gospel we'll get some idea of what we might see in evangelists today. After all, the apostles were most often those described as 'evangelising'.

A significant chapter of the Bible that condenses some of these characteristics is Acts 17. This chapter describes what the Apostle Paul did in Thessalonica, Berea and Athens and it begins with Luke using three specialist words to describe what Paul and Silas did in Thessalonica – they reasoned (v2), explained (v3) and proved (v3).

The Greek word for reasoned is *dielegeto*. It has the sense of putting forward a proposal and then dealing with objections. There's a two-way flow to this communication.

The Greek word for explained is *dianoigōn*. Literally, this means 'opening up'. It has the sense of revealing something for the first time. So, in this context you have Paul showing the Jews the evidence from Scripture concerning a suffering Messiah.

The Greek word for proved is *paratithemenos*. Literally, this means 'to place alongside'. Here it has the idea of truth being set before enquiring minds. And in this context we find Paul placing misconceptions or prejudices alongside the truth. He places the prophecies of a suffering Messiah alongside the fulfilment found in Christ.

What's fascinating about Acts 17 is that we then see this varied approach being repeated when Paul travels on to Athens.

'So he reasoned in the synagogue with both Jews and God-fearing Greeks' (v17a). Here Paul is once again proving that Jesus was the fulfilment of all the Messiah prophecies.

'A group of Epicurean and Stoic philosophers began to debate with him' (v18a). Now here Paul engages in dialogue with ordinary pagans and thinkers using a method of 'Question and Answer' that had been championed by the great Athenian philosopher Socrates.

'They took him and brought him to a meeting of the Areopagus, where they said to him, "May we know what this new teaching is that you are presenting?"' (v19). So here Paul is given an opportunity to make a presentation to the intelligentsia, the academics, the professional thinkers and philosophers of the city.

And it's my contention that evangelists have an especial gifting to use all these opportunities. They know how to provoke and then engage in debate. They're gifted in apologetics, as they defend the truth claims of the gospel. They can readily use cultural arguments to bring in God's truth (as we see Paul doing with his quotations – Acts 17:28).

I'm certainly not saying that non-evangelists can't do these things but I am suggesting that evangelists have a giftedness from Christ that makes them particularly effective in these public events and with those they have never met before. You're probably thinking right now of some evangelists you know who do this brilliantly. Well, praise God. Pray for them and ask God to gift many more!

It therefore shouldn't surprise us that the one named evangelist in the New Testament – Philip – should demonstrate this gifting in the way he not only proclaimed Christ in Samaria but also in the way he left the mini-revival that had broken out and went south onto the desert road to Gaza. And there he did what evangelists do. He made an opportunity to talk to the Ethiopian Chancellor of the Exchequer, and then grasped his chance to unpack Old Testament prophecies about Jesus, leading to the salvation and baptism of this eunuch.

So are we all evangelists? No – evangelist is a special people gift to the church from Christ. We're not all evangelists any more than we're all called to preach and teach. But we're all called to evangelise – that's something else, so I needn't beat myself up that I don't display these distinctive and varied gifts, whether that's public proclamation, group debate, apologetic presentation or personal witness out of nothing. And evangelists, be careful that you don't expect every other believer to be just like you. We have a different calling.

Chapter Four

Professionals and programmes

The circus had come to town (well, Clapham Common to be precise) and the posters had gone up in every convenience store in the locality. 'Roll up, roll up!' shouted the ringmaster as we wandered over. 'Come and see the greatest show around'. So we did. I think it was fun. All I can remember is the smell of captive animals.

The following evening we did as we had always done. We went to the Sunday night gospel service. And my father preached his heart out as only a passionate Celt could. I felt I'd been saved all over again. How could anyone not respond to such good news? And glancing around the congregation I looked to see if there were any people I didn't recognise, any sinners in need of saving, any souls engaging with the issues of eternity. Because that's how they got saved – at the event, at the Sunday night gospel service, under the power of oratory and the weight of emotion. And we knew it was our job to get them in. That's how evangelism was done. That's how sinners were saved.

And they were! So much of our 'evangelism' centred on the event. 'Roll up, roll up for the greatest show in town'. Sometimes there were gospel events arranged in our locality, sometimes in the city centre, sometimes they were part of a larger 'celebrity' driven programme. And our task was to get people in. That's what evangelism was about. That's what we advertised in the magazines and flyers we gave out. That's what our conversation centred on around the doors. Get them into the building and let the professional preacher do the rest. And we'd certainly hope that the programme wouldn't let us down. We often needed some bait to get the people in, and if that could be a converted sports star / musician / actor all the better. Or maybe someone who'd been in the news for some tragic event. That was an even bigger draw. But if anyone asked a question about what we believed, the response tended to be to get them to hear what the professional would say. They knew what to say and how to answer. They were better at it than we were.

Now please don't imagine that I'm attacking and deriding the gospel event. I sincerely believe that the 'event' can be an immensely useful way of presenting the gospel's big picture. And I believe that real-life stories help anchor gospel truths to everyday living. When the Bible is opened and faithfully taught, then inevitably there will be a variety of applications that point, in one way or another, to Christ. Please God raise up more and more gifted evangelists and proclaimers.

Indeed, it would appear that when we read about 'preaching' in the New Testament it always seems to be referring to gospel proclamation, in contrast to 'teaching' which is all about instructing believers.

The Greek word '*kerusso*', which is generally translated as preach or proclaim, occurs sixty-one times in the New Testament and is invariably used in the context of announcing the good news of Christ's work and rule. It therefore follows that there is an intimate link between the work of the evangelist and the work of preaching. This certainly helps us understand what Paul is getting at when he instructs Timothy to 'preach the word' (2 Tim. 4:2) and 'do the work of an evangelist' (2 Tim. 4:5). These are both closely interrelated.

Perhaps we have inadvertently done a mash-up with the titles 'evangelist' and 'pastor-teacher' and a clearer understanding of the biblical titles might help us avoid some of the confusion that has entered into the evangelical scene. To 'preach the word' is not shorthand for a general expository teaching ministry but rather for proclaiming the gospel word.

But hear me when I suggest that maybe there has been an over-emphasis on the building-centred event that has been to the detriment of every believers' gospel witness and responsibility. Even Colin Marshall and Tony Payne, in their excellent book *The Trellis and the Vine,* suggest 'If all the members of your congregation are given the opportunity to be trained in evangelism, more unbelievers will attend our events'.[3]

No doubt there are many reasons why the 'event' seems to be the central strategy in so much 'evangelism'. Growing church staff numbers with their ensuing specialities tend to lift responsibilities off the 'laity' and onto the professionals. The professionals in turn feel the need to produce and manage impressive set-piece events, and the money-draining building has to be more widely used to justify its existence as a meeting place for God's people.

But I'm generalising. The question I want to pose is what does the Bible really teach about how you and I should be showing and sharing the good news of Jesus? Is our job just to get people into a building to hear a gospel presentation or is there more to it than that?

Chapter Five

Being ready

'It is somewhat surprising that the New Testament contains relatively few exhortations for ordinary believers to speak the gospel to others'.[4] So observe Colin Marshall and Tony Payne in *The Trellis and the Vine*.

They're right. But it's no more surprising than the fact that very few of us have had any instruction on how to breathe. It's something that comes naturally. It's what we do. And in the same way, sharing and spreading the wonderful news of God's grace is expected to be the most natural and normal thing for any believer to do. The problem is we've made it into something that it isn't. It's become complicated, programmatic, systematised.

In fact, there are only two verses throughout the New Testament that refer specifically to how every Christian (not just evangelists) should share the good news. (By the way, we'll take some time in a later chapter to go through all the 'background' texts that fill out these two references.)

The first is Colossians 4:2-6:

Devote yourselves to prayer, being watchful and thankful. And pray for us, too, that God may open a door for our message, so that we may proclaim the mystery of Christ, for which I am in chains. Pray that I may proclaim it clearly, as I should. Be wise in the way you act towards outsiders; make the most of every opportunity. Let your

conversation be always full of grace, seasoned with salt,
so that you may know how to answer everyone.

Paul has been writing to the Colossians about his own public
ministry of gospel preaching. But he changes emphasis as he
goes on to encourage them to use every opportunity that they
have to share Christ. Not in the direct way that he uses, but in
a responsive manner – 'make the most of every opportunity.
Let your conversation be always full of grace, seasoned with
salt, so that you may know how to answer everyone'.

And this didn't seem to be just Paul's pet idea; Peter
mentions it too: 'But in your hearts set apart Christ as Lord.
Always be prepared to give an answer to everyone who asks
you to give the reason for the hope that you have. But do this
with gentleness and respect' (1 Pet. 3:15).

And what I want to suggest is that the biblical pattern for
evangelism is that every believer should be ready to respond
to every opportunity that comes their way to speak of Christ.
They don't need to manipulate or force the opening; they can
wait for God to give it to them.

I believe this is biblically consistent. This fits in with the
big sweeping story of God's salvation plan on several levels.

Firstly, it recognises God's sovereignty. No one can be saved
unless God moves in the first place. Spiritually dead corpses
have no power to decide for Jesus. Because he's in control we
can expect that he's able to move in our neighbour or colleague's
life, so that questions are asked that give us an opportunity to
share the good news about Christ.

Secondly, it leads us to prayer. As we're dependent upon
God for these openings, rather than our own ingenuity or
nerve, we're forced back to seek him for such opportunities.
I'll spend more time in his presence than in working out how
I might force an opening.

Thirdly, it encourages holy living and loving action. Holy
living is inextricably tied up with responsive evangelism.
What creates the questions in people's minds is the deliciously

distinctive lives we lead as believers, and the lovingly practical ways we do them good. 'Why are you different? Why do you tick as you do? Why are you so caring? Why are you doing those things that help us?'

Indeed, the reason we may have so few opportunities to share the good news about Christ isn't to do with the fact that we haven't the right strategies or sufficient courage; it's to do with the fact that our lives are no different to others: they're compromised, they're unattractive. Little wonder, therefore, that Paul's opening words to the Colossians in this section on evangelism are 'Be wise in the way you act towards outsiders'. And we'll look at this in more depth in a subsequent chapter.

Fourthly, it develops a Christian mindset. There are many opportunities that arise in the natural course of conversation at work, or over the garden fence, or in the shops. Someone asks you what you think about the latest story in the paper, or on some particular topical issue. As a Christian you will have a perspective that is likely to be radically different, a viewpoint that will challenge the materialism or relativism of the age. Increasingly a mind that understands and is shaped by God's truth will clash with the presuppositions of today's society.

Little wonder Paul tells the Colossian believers 'Let your conversation be always full of grace, seasoned with salt' (Col. 4:6), and little wonder we'll need to return to this theme later.

But then this approach is not only biblically consistent, it's also practically wise. And these two categories go together. We're convinced that the Bible, the living Word of the living God, is radically relevant. And this comes over in a number of ways.

Firstly, it removes strain and false guilt. Because if evangelism is down to me forcing an opening, then there'll always be pressure to manipulate situations. And if I find at the end of the day that I haven't been able to present the major points of the gospel I'll feel the guilt of failure. But when I'm waiting for the opportunity that God provides, I can rest in his providence and timing. I'm not going to get upset if, on a particular occasion, the chance hasn't arisen to share Christ. I'll rest in God's sovereignty and wait for another opportunity.

Secondly, it encourages excellence in our tasks. For God calls me to do whatever task I have to the very best of my abilities. And, therefore, I'll concentrate on those tasks without worrying about manufacturing a situation for sharing Christ. I can leave that in his hands. And, until such an opportunity arises, I'll do what I have to do as well as I can and get God the glory through that.

Thirdly, it develops genuine friendships. You probably know some Christians who always feel the duty to blast anyone they meet with the gospel as soon as they can. They maybe get a reputation at work. And the outcome is they're known as Bible thumpers and are generally avoided as religious weirdos. They haven't had the opportunity to develop the friendships that more naturally, in God's gracious timing, will lead to profitable sharing of Christ.

I think one of the most important lessons I've learnt is that we should love people for who they are, and trust that at just the right time in that friendship, the Lord will provide the opportunity to speak for him. I no longer look upon those I meet as potential gospel projects but as men and women created in the image of God, blessed by common grace but lost in their sin and needing the Saviour.

Fourthly, it allows effective, relaxed and open conversations. Because when I respond to others, I am not intruding into their space. Rather, they've chosen the time, the place and the subject. They're relaxed, they're enquiring, and therefore they're more open than when I might go in with all guns blazing at a time that might be inconvenient, upon a subject that might not be touching their major need of that moment. If they ask the question, they've invited me to share what I believe, and, in presenting Christ, I am legitimately responding to what they have asked.

And fifthly, it embraces all personality types. The danger with imagining that evangelism is exclusively about forcing situations to share Christ is that some people will inevitably back off and do nothing. They feel uncomfortable with such an approach. It's so alien to their nature. And yet when my responsibility is to respond to the opportunities that God sovereignly provides, then I'm being invited to be me and to share honestly and openly how Jesus Christ impacts my life. Such an approach involves every believer. It excludes none.

Well, that's the big idea in summary form. I'm trying to contend that evangelism is far more natural than many specialists would have us believe. Above all, I'm suggesting that this is what the Bible actually teaches. We don't need to be governed by the latest theory or methodology. What we really need is to be gripped by the stunning grace of Christ and live our lives under his beautiful Lordship and rule. And as that becomes more and more real in our lives, we won't think twice about sharing Jesus. It will be as natural as breathing.

Chapter Six

Bible-shaped gospel work

Our passion must not be whether a thing works, but whether it is what Scripture commends or commands. So, we must ask the question – does the growth of the early church, recorded for us in Acts and illustrated in the New Testament letters, reflect the distinction between the work of evangelists and the responsibilities of all God's children?

For the Apostle Paul there was nothing more important than 'preaching the gospel'. In the Greek language this is captured in one word – *euangelizomai* (εὐαγγελίζομαι), from which we get the noun / verb 'evangelism / evangelise'. When Paul uses this word it always carries with it the sense of primary gospel announcement (with the possible exception of Rom. 1:15) and he uses it in connection with himself, other apostles and a recognised band of evangelists.

So, does Paul extend the use of this word *euangelizomai* to all believers? Of the sixty-eight occurrences of this word, only twenty are in the context of non-evangelists, and of these the vast bulk describe how the believers *received* the gospel through the proclamation of Paul and his co-workers. John Dickson, in his thesis – *Mission Commitment in Ancient Judaism and in the Pauline Communities* – convincingly argues that the language describing apostolic evangelism is not used of believers in the same way. He concludes 'Nowhere are believers portrayed as responsible for or engaged in the task of proclaiming of the gospel. One cannot avoid the impression that Paul did not understand his converts' role in the advancement of the gospel as the same as, or even as similar to, his own'.[5]

We should therefore expect to find references to these evangelists who were recognised for their ministry of 'gospel proclamation'. And we do.

In 2 Corinthians 8:18 we read 'And we are sending along with him the brother who is praised by all the churches for his service to the gospel'.

And here we find again that word – *'euangelion'* (εὐαγγελίῳ). So, it appears that this famous brother is someone recognised by the local churches as an evangelist. Indeed, it is argued that the 'apostles (representatives) of the churches' mentioned just a few verses later in 8:23 are also to be understood as gospel proclaimers who are recognised by the churches.

Philippians 4:2-3 says:

> I plead with Euodia and I plead with Syntyche to be of the same mind in the Lord. Yes, and I ask you, my true companion, help these women since they have contended at my side in the cause of the gospel, along with Clement and the rest of my co-workers, whose names are in the book of life.

Here these two women are identified as those who worked with Paul in the cause of the gospel (εὐαγγελίῳ) along with Clement and other unnamed co-workers. Dickson's observation is that 'Paul's continuing willingness to describe them as co-workers and to ascribe to them the traditional honorific … strongly suggests that these men and women were continuing to struggle together in the proclamation of the gospel in and around Philippi'.[6]

This also helps explain an earlier reference in this letter that at first glance might seem to suggest that formal, proclamatory evangelism is something to be undertaken by all believers.

> And because of my chains, most of the brothers and sisters have become confident in the Lord and dare all the more to proclaim the gospel (εὐαγγέλιον) without fear (Phil. 1:14).

But in the Greek 'the brothers' has a more specific and technical definition. Dickson quotes E.E. Ellis: 'When used in the plural with an article, "the brothers" in Pauline literature fairly consistently refers to a relatively limited group of workers, some of who have the Christian mission and / or ministry as their primary occupation'.[7]

Dickson's summary is 'During the course of his missionizing activity in an area, Paul's normative expectation was that certain men and women among his converts (or his missionary team) would further the work of local evangelisation once he had departed'.[8]

So, what we are suggesting? Namely that there is a clear distinction between the work of evangelists and the work of evangelising by non-evangelists which seems to be borne out by the biblical record. But it does beg the question – so what were non-evangelists expected to do? How did Paul expect his converts to give themselves to the promotion of the gospel? And once again we have to say that the New Testament is not silent on this issue.

1. Money

However distasteful or grubby this might sound to our ears (especially when associated with the money-grabbing tactics of some hypocritical TV evangelists) the reality remains – gospel work requires funding and support. And Paul is not ashamed to face up to this and encourage both churches and individuals to be active in giving to gospel ministry.

It would seem that Paul viewed this financial support in three ways. Firstly, what a congregation pays a worker whilst he is among them; secondly, the travel expenses that would help the worker as he moves on to his next location; and thirdly money that is given for 'missionary' work when the worker isn't present with that congregation.

Let's take each in turn.

Living expenses

Paul assumes that churches should pay for the gospel workers who come amongst them (1 Thess. 2:1-9; 2 Thess. 3:8; 1 Cor. 9:1-18) although, for various reasons, he himself did not always make use of such provision (1 Cor. 9:18; 1 Thess. 2:9).

Sending expenses

In five places Paul makes reference to churches 'sending' workers on their way (1 Cor. 16:6, 11; 2 Cor. 1:16; Rom. 15:24; Titus 3:13). The Greek word he uses (προπέμπω, *propempo*) carries the sense of equipping, both with resources and personnel. For example, when Paul writes to the church at Rome it would seem his overarching purpose is to secure, in advance, support for the mission he wanted to undertake in Spain, that he would collect when he arrived from Jerusalem.

Missionary expenses

Paul speaks about this to the Philippian church, thanking them for their help in supporting his missionary work in general (Phil. 4:10-19). This was a love-gift from that church, rather than a demand or expectation. In fact, it may be these gifts from Philippi which enabled Paul not to be a financial burden to the young churches at Corinth and Thessalonica.

So, let's try and earth all this for ourselves. How can we help advance the gospel if we are not 'evangelists'? Well, one significant, vital and often overlooked element is that we should be generous givers. Gospel work requires resources, and through sacrificial giving God's people enable that work to go forward.

2. Prayer

To suggest that prayer is essential in gospel work seems so commonplace that one might yawn and pass this section by. Sadly, however, it would seem this is what happens in so much church life today – believers pass by the prayer meeting and fail to engage in prayer for the lost. We can read books about strategy, we put in place impressive seminars, we show all the latest training DVDs but we fail to engage in prayer. But an examination of the New Testament record reveals how integral prayer was to the expansion of the early church.

Prayer for unbelievers in general
We see something of Paul's passion for the lost when he shares an insight into his own heart with the believers in Rome. Talking about his own national people he writes this – 'Brothers and sisters, my heart's desire and prayer to God for the Israelites is that they may be saved' (Rom. 10:1). And it wasn't just that Paul prayed for Israel, he wanted all the churches to be praying for all the people. Writing to Timothy he urges that 'petitions, prayers, intercession and thanksgiving be made for all people—for kings and all those in authority, that we may live peaceful and quiet lives in all godliness and holiness. This is good, and pleases God our Saviour, who wants all people to be saved and to come to a knowledge of the truth' (1 Tim. 2:1-4).

And when you look at the context of these verses you discover that Paul is not concerned primarily with a well-ordered, civic society, but that through the peace that good government brings, believers will be able to lead God-honouring and distinctive lives (vv 8-10), pointing many to saving faith in Christ.

So, prayer for the lost was a feature of the early church. They wanted to align their hearts with God's saving purposes. And this continued. Ignatius of Antioch, writing sometime around AD 98-117, encouraged Christian communities to go on doing this. 'Now for other men pray unceasingly, for there is in them a hope of repentance, that they may find God' (Ignatius, Eph.10.1).

My own experience has been that churches who are passionate to see the lost saved and let that passion overflow in corporate prayer are churches who regularly see unbelievers come to faith in Jesus.

Prayer for gospel opportunities in particular
Paul often requested prayer for himself and his band of gospel workers as they carried out their work.

> Brothers and sisters, pray for us (1 Thess. 5:25).

> As for other matters, brothers and sisters, pray for us that the message of the Lord may spread rapidly and be honoured, just as it was with you (2 Thess. 3:1).

> Devote yourselves to prayer, being watchful and thankful. And pray for us, too, that God may open a door for our message, so that we may proclaim the mystery of Christ, for which I am in chains. Pray that I may proclaim it clearly, as I should (Col. 4:2-4).

> Pray also for me, that whenever I speak, words may be given me so that I will fearlessly make known the mystery of the gospel, for which I am an ambassador in chains. Pray that I may declare it fearlessly, as I should (Eph. 6:19-20).

Little wonder Gordon Wiles, in *Paul's Intercessory Prayers*, says this: 'Prayer buttressed all his mission work – in advance of his visits, during them, and after he had departed ... Taken together, then, the intercessory prayer passages offer impressive documentation of Paul's unfailing reliance upon the ministry of supplication, his own and that of his fellow believers'.[9]

So what should non-evangelists do? Part of that answer is clearly that they should give financially towards gospel work and they should pray for it, both in its broadest context (with a heart that shares God's passion for the lost) and also with insight and discernment. Paul's instruction to the Colossian church to be watchful implies that we should be aware of some of the situations facing those engaged as evangelists. This might well mean following prayer updates and prayer letters produced by such workers and praying faithfully through them.

The danger we face as we conclude this chapter is that we're more preoccupied with quick-fix strategies and inspirational ideas than with the sacrificial expectations of knuckling down to giving and prayer. Before we go on to examine the role that non-evangelists play in the world today, we need to stop at this point and see if our evangelistic seriousness is matched by our commitment in these two areas.

Chapter Seven

Living in the material world

My parents were some of the greatest and godliest people I have known. It was an immense privilege growing up in that Christian home. But there were some rules, designed (or at least that's how it seemed to me) to keep us hermetically sealed off from 'the world' and the contamination that could bring. So we didn't play cards, go to the cinema, visit the theatre, play outside on a Sunday, dance, eat at restaurants or drink alcohol. I did, however, attend five church services on a Sunday wearing my 'Sunday best'.

Music was okay, as long as it was pre-1950. We were about the last family in the district to get a stereo record player, and then the only records we borrowed from the library were from the classical music section. And as my sense of puzzlement and rebellion grew, along with my hair, I remember buying my first-ever album, the progrockers, Emerson Lake and Palmer with their 'Pictures at an Exhibition', explaining to my mother that it was based on Mussorgsky's wonderful classical suite – although I don't think my dad ever worked out how 'Nut Rocker' (the final track) fitted into that musical genre.

Sport was all right. In fact, it was positively encouraged. But I remember when the coach carrying the school team stopped at a pub, I saw it as my Christian duty to stay in the coach and not venture into such a worldly domain.

I understand now, looking back, why we were raised in such a fashion and the love and care that went into these 'regulations'. But its effect was to build into my psyche a suspicion of anything 'worldly'. There was a distinction that needed to be retained. We weren't of the world. We needed to remain apart and separate.

Yet it seems to be this very division that Paul is at pains to counter when he writes to the church at Corinth. It seems that some believers misunderstood what he had written in an earlier letter when he was giving instructions about church discipline, as it would appear he had counselled them not to associate with a sexually immoral church member.

'I wrote to you in my letter not to associate with sexually immoral people – not at all meaning the people of this world who are immoral, or the greedy and swindlers, or idolaters. In that case you would have to leave this world' (1 Cor. 5:9-10).

And Paul's expression – 'not at all' – carries with it a sense of astonishment that the Christians in Corinth should ever think of withdrawing from social contact with outsiders. In fact, the implication is that Paul expected them to maintain such associations. And this is borne out in later passages from 1 Corinthians where Paul talks to them about using social meals that they would have attended.

> So whether you eat or drink or whatever you do, do it all for the glory of God. Do not cause anyone to stumble, whether Jews, Greeks or the church of God – even as I try to please everyone in every way. For I am not seeking my own good but the good of many, so that they may be saved. Follow my example, as I follow the example of Christ (1 Cor. 10:31-11:1).

And that example of Christ had horrified the religious leaders of the day – 'This man welcomes sinners and eats with them' (Luke 15:2). In his gospel, Luke records so many meals at which Jesus is present that Robert Karris states: 'In Luke's

Gospel Jesus is either going to a meal, at a meal, or coming from a meal'.[10]

Meals were the natural means for social interaction, and Paul wanted the Corinthian believers to use those opportunities wisely. Some of these meals were primarily religious, and their close connection to idolatrous practices meant he issued words of warning (1 Cor. 10:14-22) but with other meals in Corinth (1 Cor. 8; 10:27-11:1) Paul hoped that the believers would intentionally engage with their pagan neighbours, in the hope that their distinctive and godly lifestyle would win them a hearing.

The 'contamination' that Paul encouraged was not that of the 'world' infecting holy living, but rather the loving integrity of the Christian community challenging pagan suppositions.

For some of us today this interaction can indeed be over a meal, where in a relaxed context we are able to share our lives as well as our food. But let's not forget that dining rooms and dining tables are the preserve of only certain sections of society. Many would be deeply uncomfortable to come to a meal and talk around a table when their own background is that of eating food in front of a television, and certainly not having a conversation in the process. We need to be sensitive to our contexts and discover natural ways to interact with our neighbourhood. It may be the local pub or club; it may mean getting involved in community issues or sporting clubs; it might be a reading group or with an am-dram society. Whatever it is, there are many good and legitimate ways we can naturally interact with others and celebrate with them God's common grace (although they may not initially see it in that way!).

The danger is that we fall into the Christian ghetto mentality. We prefer our own less challenging and uncontaminated Christian space. We look to our own comforts. We fill our week with Christian meeting after Christian meeting. We take a perverse pride that we are so busy in the Lord's work. We manage to live life in the bubble and avoid any of the messy realities that come with a sin-stained world.

I still remember the moment. It burnt into my pastor's conscience like hydrofluoric acid. We'd hired a boat in the city centre and engaged a winsome evangelist to speak. But as the day drew nearer the tickets weren't being taken up and we had to cancel. Why? I launched an investigation and the answer came back – 'we don't have unbelieving friends'. We had great training programmes; our small groups were running well and a variety of committees kept the church operating efficiently. In fact, I almost felt guilty as a pastor if we hadn't laid on one activity or another throughout the week. But many of the church members had no meaningful contact with unsaved people. We'd built the ghetto without realising.

And so began the process of reshaping church life so that it no longer revolved around us – the Christians – but around our friends, neighbours and colleagues who were being robbed of life without Christ. We cleared days in the week when no meetings were to be held and set them aside for meeting others. We refocused our attention on those outside the Christian community, not those within. We did fewer big, set-piece events, and encouraged more one-to-one relationship building.

May I ask how you're doing in this area? If I asked you to list half a dozen unchurched friends, could you? And what about community activities? Where are you meeting others outside your church life? The lie many of us have fallen into is that evangelism is done in a church building by professional staff. And, sadly, this is unthinkingly propagated by so many writers and evangelists (I have their books piled up on my desk as I type).

Dave Kinnaman and Gabe Lyons published some research in their book *unChristian* which illustrates this problem.

In our interviews, a twenty-eight-year-old Christian described this lifestyle: "So many Christians are caught up in the Christian subculture and are completely closed off from the world. We go to church on Wednesdays, Sundays, and sometimes on Saturdays. We attend small group on Tuesday night and serve on the Sunday school advisory board, the financial committee, and the welcoming committee. We go to barbeques with our Christian friends and plan group outings. We are closed off from the world. Even if we wanted to reach out to non-Christians, we don't have time and we don't know how. The only way we know how to reach out is to invite people to join in our Christian social circle".[11]

Repeated statistical evidence reveals that the overwhelming majority of people who come to faith from outside a Christian family do so not as a result of a church meeting but because of getting to know a real Christian. It's time we learnt this lesson – it's biblical after all!

Chapter Eight

Deliciously distinctive

Although Christians occasionally get together (usually on a Sunday) in a home, hall or some building they might have built or bought, the vast majority of the time the church is scattered throughout a community, living in apartments and flats, houses, caravans, bungalows or mansions. And the biblical expectation now, as it was in Paul's day, is that there should be an evangelistic lifestyle.

Here's Paul writing to the Christians in Thessalonica – 'make it your ambition to lead a quiet life: You should mind your own business and work with your hands, just as we told you, so that your daily life may win the respect of outsiders and so that you will not be dependent on anybody' (1 Thess. 4:11-12).

Now remember this was a church that had a tough start – 'severe suffering' (1:6); 'you suffered from your own people' (2:14); 'unsettled by these trials' (3:3). But Paul expects that they won't retaliate against the way they were treated by unbelieving neighbours but would work for peace instead. What's more, he expects that a lifestyle which is peaceful, non-interfering and self-sufficient will be attractive to the wider society, where such characteristics are rarely seen, though often desired.

That's probably what Paul was getting at when writing to the Philippians – 'Let your gentleness be evident to all' (Phil. 4:5). Although the English translation seems somewhat bland, the force of the Greek suggests that the believers were to express 'graciousness' toward an unbelieving, undeserving and, at times, hostile society. And as such a lifestyle is seen, it would complement the gospel message being shared by the evangelists in that area.

Back in Chapter Four I suggested that one of the key passages we need to get our heads (and hearts) around is Colossians 4:2-6. This is a key section that brings together many of the themes we're looking at in this book. And I mentioned that we'd need to return to what it says about wise and distinctive living.

Let's lay it out again – 'Devote yourselves to prayer, being watchful and thankful. And pray for us, too, that God may open a door for our message, so that we may proclaim the mystery of Christ, for which I am in chains. Pray that I may proclaim it clearly, as I should. Be wise in the way you act towards outsiders; make the most of every opportunity. Let your conversation be always full of grace, seasoned with salt, so that you may know how to answer everyone'.

Notice the connection between Paul's gospel proclamation and the life of the believers. Having requested prayer for his own ministry he immediately goes on to tell the Colossian Christians that their conduct should be 'wise' before an unbelieving world. In the context this seems to imply that the instructions for godly living which are outlined in chapter 3:1-4:1 are to be worked through in such a way that a pagan audience will take note, that the proclaimed gospel will find an open door, and that questions will be provoked enabling believers to point to Christ.

And there should be a positive grasping of every opportunity. The Greek text speaks of 'buying up' or 'redeeming' opportunities. Dickson says this of the passage: 'the whole phrase points to a deliberate and enthusiastic seizing of opportunities to do good deeds toward non-Christians. Seen in this light, the apostle's injunction is quite forceful in its missionary orientation: Christians are to be vigorous in their ethical apologetic'.[12]

The evangelistic nature of doing good is seen even more clearly when Paul writes to Titus, advising him what to do on the island of Crete, where ungodly behaviour was even more pronounced (Titus 1:12-14) and where false teachers were touting for adherents (1:10-11). He addresses older and younger men and women, encouraging them to integrity in all their actions, 'so that no one will malign the word of God' (2:5). Even slaves are brought into this same high ethical requirement:

> Teach slaves to be subject to their masters in everything, to try to please them, not to talk back to them, and not to steal from them, but to show that they can be fully trusted,' and the reason for this is made transparently clear – 'so that in every way they will make the teaching about God our Saviour attractive (2:9-10).

In fact, the word translated here about making the gospel 'attractive' is the one from which we get the word 'cosmetics'. So Paul is saying that the believers should live lives that will beautifully decorate and commend the good news about Jesus Christ. Against a backdrop of immoral lifestyles and heretical teaching, Paul insists that godly behaviour will beautify and commend the true gospel message. Little wonder that Paul begins to conclude his letter by emphasising gospel truths and commanding Titus – 'I want you to stress these things, so that those who have trusted in God may be careful to devote themselves to doing what is good. These things are excellent and profitable for everyone' (3:8).

In the context it may well be argued that 'everyone' refers to believers and unbelievers alike. As the Christians live out pure, kind and self-controlled lives (2:5-8) not only will they themselves be blessed but the watching community will be pointed to Christ, the one who makes such redemption and transformation possible.

We may conclude this chapter by stating as clearly as we can that Christ-honouring behaviour will have a definite evangelistic impact upon a fractured world. This behaviour was not just the absence of evil but was the very deliberate working out of good and helpful behaviour. We might suggest that just as supernatural gifts authenticated the authority of the apostolic band, so godly living authenticated the message they preached. We need to view the New Testament letters through a missiological lens. All too often the ethical implications are relegated to a lifestyle code for believers whereas they were written to be a signpost for unbelievers. Indeed, a myopia has often come across the church, blinding it to the frequent commands to do good and be a blessing to their communities.

Adolf von Harnack, the historian of church mission, concluded his famous study with the following words:

> Nevertheless, it was not merely the confessors and martyrs who were missionaries. It was characteristic of this religion that everyone who seriously confessed the faith proved of service to its propaganda. Christians were to "let their light shine, that pagans may see their good works and glorify the Father in heaven". If this dominated all their life, and if they lived according to the precepts of their religion, they could not be hidden at all; by their very mode of living they could not fail to preach their faith plainly and audibly.[13]

If we are seriously trying to work out what 'non-evangelists' do to evangelise, we have to place Jesus-shaped living towards the top of our list. And that may well be why so many of us see so few opportunities to share Christ with others. Our lives aren't different. We've so blended into the background by our contaminated and compromised living that we in no way commend glorious, radical gospel truth. Little wonder we go looking for quick-fix evangelistic strategies; little wonder there's such a market for the latest self-help guide to witnessing.

And may I add, little wonder that so many churches are so ineffective and see such little 'conversion' growth. Their focus is on the well-being and enjoyment of their members, rather than in discerning how they might bless and practically do good to the communities where they meet.

Chapter Nine

Hospitality

Middle-class 'respectability' has contaminated and compromised many areas of Christian witness. It seems at times that the house we live in and the impression we give to others matter more than the eternal destiny of the lost. And so we 'entertain' our friends in carefully choreographed events, displaying the best of who we are.

Okay, that might be a slightly unkind caricature of what happens, and, on many occasions, we enjoy genuine friendship and love, laced with laughter and fun. But there can still be a residue of respectability that holds us back from 'hospitality' – opening up our home and ourselves to the uncontrolled chaos of a family meal with both friends and strangers.

In God's goodness we are increasingly learning what true hospitality is. Thanks to books from folk like Rosaria Butterfield (*The Gospel Comes with a Housekey*) and Carolyn Lacey (*Extraordinary Hospitality*) many of us are rethinking what it means to model the grace of Christ in our homes. As Carolyn writes: 'We need to start by rejecting the world's picture of superficial hospitality. Our goal is not to show off our homes or our cooking skills (or lack of them!) but our Saviour'.[14]

In this area, as in many others, we need to deconstruct our assumptions by returning to the Bible's teaching. As Rosaria tells us 'Hospitality is the ground zero of the Christian life'.[15]

It was the means whereby she came to reconsider the truth claims of the Christian faith. As a lesbian, postmodern atheist professor she was invited into community by an older Christian couple named Ken and Floy Smith. She was deeply suspicious about Christians and the Bible and had accepted the initial invitation to discover why Christians hated her. Nonetheless, the Smiths accepted Rosaria and loved her into the kingdom. Their home became her 'refuge,' where she wrestled with the Bible and who Jesus really is.

Years later, Rosaria's family was in the same position to offer unconditional love to their neighbour Hank. She says, 'Jesus dines with sinners so that He can get close enough to touch us ... to change and transform us, so that after we have dined with Jesus, we want Jesus more than the sin that beckons us'.[16] And so she argues that we are all called to welcome fellow image-bearers into following Jesus with us – to come as they are, and go to Jesus together with us.

But so many objections instinctively arise in our hearts. On the one hand we think about all those things that we couldn't do, to which Carolyn responds '... Nowhere does [the Bible] talk about tableware or tray bakes. Neither does it link hospitality with expense, exhaustion or an extroverted personality. So I'm not going to do that either'.[17] And on the other hand we sometimes think such open-handed hospitality is below us. She writes, 'pride hinders our hospitality in two ways. On one hand it keeps us from reaching out to the people most in need of our welcome because we think that we are somehow above them. On the other hand, it inhibits us from welcoming others because we worry about what people may think of us'.[18]

What a profound difference this would make to our gospel witness if we were to show the same acceptance of others that Jesus did. What a powerful way we can identify with the stranger, the outsider and the needy. Such hospitality helps shape a distinctive Christian culture from the inside out as it embraces gospel optimism, knowing that if God sovereignly wills, strangers will become neighbours and those neighbours, by his grace, will become part of the family of God.

As Jesvin Jose concluded:

> We can be generous, compassionate, humble, persistent, aware, inclusive, and sacrificial hosts reflecting the God who shows us these same characteristics in His Word. Hospitality can indeed be a joyful pursuit. It can be a wonderful means to bless others and point them to the God who lovingly welcomes us all.[19]

Are you ready to open your home? Are you ready to partner with others if that's not a possibility? Are you ready to open your heart in this practical demonstration?

Chapter Ten

Tasty words

St Francis of Assisi never said 'Preach the gospel and if necessary use words'. It may sound clever. It may even be the fig leaf used by many an evangelical to cover over their cowardly silence when opportunities arise. But it's wrong. Distinctive gospel living must be explained and shared with distinctive gospel words. 'Life' and 'lip' go together. And nowhere is that clearer than in what are becoming our favourite verses in this book – Colossians 4:2-6, especially vv 5-6: 'Be wise in the way you act towards outsiders; make the most of every opportunity. Let your conversation be always full of grace, seasoned with salt, so that you may know how to answer everyone'.

As we have previously noted, Paul moves from instructions about prayer (especially for his own preaching) to instructions for distinctive Christian living. Believers in Colosse (and beyond) are to live in such a way that they will need speech to explain their behaviour and point to Christ. And this speech will be 'full of grace, seasoned with salt'. Although some think Paul is saying that elements of wit and wisdom should be found throughout their speech, like salt in a meal, the safer and simpler explanation is that Paul is saying that grace should be the tasty seasoning that permeates and flavours everything they say. It's not primarily here about what you say, but rather 'how' you say it. It's not primarily about the message; it's about the manner.

Now that's not to say the message isn't important, far from it, but it's not the specific point that Paul is making here. He isn't talking about public proclamation but private conversation.

It's as believers live in their communities, with all the joys and tensions that can bring, that they should naturally be communicating in ways that are grace-filled.

We need to remember that these words in Colossians chapter 4 had been preceded in chapter 3 by some strong words of command and encouragement to the believing community. Listen to how they were to live and speak:

> But now you must rid yourselves of all such things as these: anger, rage, malice, slander, and filthy language from your lips. Do not lie to each other, since you have taken off your old self with its practices and have put on the new self, which is being renewed in knowledge in the image of its Creator. Here there is no Greek or Jew, circumcised or uncircumcised, barbarian, Scythian, slave or free, but Christ is all, and is in all. Therefore, as God's chosen people, holy and dearly loved, clothe yourselves with compassion, kindness, humility, gentleness and patience. Bear with each other and forgive whatever grievances you may have against one another. Forgive as the Lord forgave you. And over all these virtues put on love, which binds them all together in perfect unity. Let the peace of Christ rule in your hearts, since as members of one body you were called to peace. And be thankful. Let the word of Christ dwell in you richly as you teach and admonish one another with all wisdom, and as you sing psalms, hymns and spiritual songs with gratitude in your hearts to God. And whatever you do, whether in word or deed, do it all in the name of the Lord Jesus, giving thanks to God the Father through him (Col. 3:8-17).

And I make that at least ten references to various forms of speech. It's in a following chapter that we see these 'ethical' commands have an outward-looking orientation. Why speak and behave like this? It's so that others will be drawn to Christ. This isn't just about the Christian community retaining a distinctive purity for its own good (although that will be an undoubted side effect) but so that others will become aware of the relevant and radical difference that being a follower of Jesus Christ makes.

Of course, this is the same point that Peter makes in the verses that precede his call for gospel readiness. He is passionately concerned that believers should use their speech in such a way that commends their Christian profession. He begins by quoting from Psalm 34:

> 'Whoever would love life
>   and see good days
>   must keep their tongue from evil
>   and their lips from deceitful speech.
> They must turn from evil and do good;
>   they must seek peace and pursue it.
> For the eyes of the Lord are on the righteous
>   and his ears are attentive to their prayer,
>   but the face of the Lord is against those who do evil'.

> ... But in your hearts revere Christ as Lord. Always be prepared to give an answer to everyone who asks you to give the reason for the hope that you have. But do this with gentleness and respect (1 Pet. 3:10-12, 15).

And it's no surprise that in his letter James speaks often about the dangers of the tongue. He'd come to hear how the behaviour of many was contradicting the truth of the gospel and so he implores them to use their words carefully. And such a corrective is needed today as Christians are not generally known for their gracious speech. Some are better at judgement than grace. Some approve of street preachers who are arrested for homophobic comments, spoken (or so it seems) in a desire to enforce Christendom values rather than to win hearts and minds. Spittle-filled rage at Pride rallies, declaring that 'queers go to hell' doesn't seem the best way to commend the gospel message in its entirety.

My wake-up call to this teaching came as I angrily shut the door on the latest couple of Jehovah's Witnesses. My arguments against their false teaching had been great. I marshalled my knowledge of Greek, history and theology and demolished their heretical suggestions, but grew in anger and frustration as they refused to see the sheer logic of what I'd put before them, culminating in a less than gracious parting on the doorstep.

But as the door slammed shut I reflected that although I'd won the argument I hadn't won their hearts. My abrasive manner contradicted the very love of which I had been speaking, and so I determined in the future to speak respectfully, gently and graciously to such callers, carefully suggesting that further investigation on the internet might give them more insight into the points I was making. (Although the change in tactics of this movement, away from house calling to stalls near major urban hubs has somewhat limited my new resolution!)

In fact, this characteristic of gracious, respectful and gentle speech should mark all our interactions. As Christians are pressured to conform to the new standards imposed upon them by the secular elites, our responses will stand out in sharp contrast to the dogmatism, arrogance and bile that sometimes gets directed towards Bible believers. Rather than buckle in a cowed silence, we have an opportunity to speak truth with dignified restraint, not rising to the barbs of the 'thought police'.

But let's face it, the reality is that for most of us our interactions are with friends, colleagues and family. These are not confrontational situations; these are times when living under the Lordship of Christ will naturally overflow in our comments and observations. We'll talk about going to church as naturally as we would attending a concert; we'll be full of gratitude for things that have happened to us; we'll offer to pray into a tough situation our friend is facing; we'll be honest and open about our own brokenness and experience of grace. In other words, Jesus will litter our conversations both in the words we use and the way we speak them.

And let's not limit our communication just to spoken words. In our social media obsessed age, what we write or share on some of these platforms also speaks volumes about the reality of the gospel in our lives. We need always to have an intentionality about what we share. Too often believers can be compromised by those throwaway, careless comments that litter Twitter and Facebook, and by detracting trivialities. We live out the glory, joy and seriousness of our faith as much in these 'virtual' contexts as in our physical interactions.

Employers are increasingly using the Facebook contributions of a prospective employee to assess their suitability or otherwise. It gives them an insight not only into what that person does but how that person reacts; it provides a window into their personalities. I'm just fearful that some believers are better known for their political views or sporting affiliations than for their Christian profession, that they are more concerned with promoting their own prejudices than with commending their Saviour.

Chapter Eleven

The church as community

I grew up in the age of 'object lessons'. I still remember some of the children's talks that my father gave: four-foot-high traffic lights, a large ship's wheel, a giant weighing-scale, a cross with a 'bronze' snake wrapped around it. And I can even remember some of the lessons they were illustrating! Of course, we don't see many of these today. Kids are far more sophisticated, and these clunky structures don't compare well alongside the smooth video displays on the apps and iPads that they've grown up with. (I'm still waiting for flannelgraphs to make a comeback. Yes – you read it here first!)

But 'object lessons' still have a vital role to play in communicating the gospel. Not just things like the 'wordless book' with its many symbolic colours, but above all the local church with its motley collection of broken but saved individuals, gathering together to hear and respond to God and his Word, gathering to encourage one another, gathering to worship and wonder at the saving grace that brought them together in the first place. The most radical, welcoming, countercultural community you could ever find in a secular society – the most diverse, barrier-busting bunch you could hope to meet (or at least that's how it should be).

Little wonder that in his book, *Church Planting for a Greater Harvest*, C. Peter Wagner wrote: 'The single most effective evangelistic methodology under heaven is planting new churches'.[20]

For it's in the church that gospel truths are most clearly seen. In a fractured and divided world there is something glorious about experiencing unity across generational, ethnic and social divides. It's a foretaste of heaven. It's something we were made for and that we ache after. And it's not surprising that many seekers find that church life not only confirms the gospel truths they've been hearing but also resonates with that deep-seated longing for home that has been buried inside.

Now you and I know that not every church is like that. Broken and selfish people are not made perfect overnight, and churches at times can look more like battlegrounds than gardens of grace. But with God's help in the power of the Holy Spirit working through the Word of God, the life of Jesus can be seen to a greater or lesser degree amongst his people. When we speak of the 'body of Christ' we mean that Jesus can indeed be seen through his people and through those object lessons of communion and baptism.

And there's a particular way that church speaks into today's society – it gives an antidote to the loneliness epidemic that is sweeping through the west. Recent polls from YouGov and others found that 30 per cent of millennials (those born between 1981 and 1995) say they feel lonely. Furthermore, 22 per cent of millennials say they have zero friends. 27 per cent said they have 'no close friends,' 30 per cent said they have 'no best friends,' and 25 per cent said they have no acquaintances. (Whatever that means!)

It seems the same levels (if not higher) are being reported for Gen Z (those born between 1997 and 2012) and that loneliness tends to increase markedly after age seventy-five. For all the good that social media can do in connecting lonely people, it seems the overall effect of spending more time on the internet is to isolate one person from another.

This is where the church must be the church! If ever there should be a welcoming, inclusive community it should be the gathered company of God's people: men and women reaching out with warmth and joy, sharing food with one another, delighting to welcome and receive other broken sinners like themselves, overflowing with the beautiful grace of Jesus Christ.

But the gathered church fulfils another function. Sam Chan speaks about plausibility structures in his excellent book, *Evangelism in a Skeptical World.* He points out that in our age communities have a powerful role in helping form beliefs, and that the gathering of people to celebrate the life, death and resurrection of Jesus Christ can begin to subvert the preconceptions of many who have too quickly bought into the narrative of the age.

This is why every city, town or village should have a gospel church. It's not only for the convenience of the believers (who for the most part are sufficiently mobile to travel to another centre for their 'church' if they so wished) but to be a gospel signpost, an object lesson, to the reality of the new life that Christ offers. And lest our mental image of church is instinctively a special building in which Christians gather only on a Sunday, we need to revisit our theological roots and understand that believers can come together on any day, in any place under the Word of God and be that church which reflects the glory of Jesus. A village may be too small to sustain a special building and a dedicated pastor, but during the week God's people can get together in a family home, and God's Word can be shared by appropriately gifted individuals. Even there, as friends are invited, gospel truths can be on display, complementing the verbal proclamation.

That's why I've considered it one of the privileges of my life to be the FIEC Mission Director for over ten years and to have had an especial responsibility to encourage and facilitate the planting of new gospel churches throughout the UK. I've loved to see the courage and creativity that's gone into these new churches. I've loved to see the vision of established churches identifying areas where the gospel needs to be heard and seen. I've loved to see the commitment of core groups of believers to leave their existing church to help establish a witness elsewhere. I've loved to see the imagination that's gone into planting a church into areas that are culturally distinct or geographically challenging. I've loved the sacrifice that all this has entailed and yet the willingness and boldness to move forward in dependence upon God.

Maybe God is calling you to go in this way. Whatever our situation we know that we need to be ready to share our lives with other believers in such a way that reveals Jesus. The rugged individuality, so prized by Western culture, has little place in this picture. Rather, communities of grace seeking to build one another up under the Word of God will continue to be that central tool in the purposes of God.

Chapter Twelve

Who's in charge?

You may call it the elephant in the room; I call it the most delightful and encouraging news there is. It's this – God's in control of all things, and that includes the salvation and rescue of lost, helpless, hell-bound people.

Barnabas and Paul had set out on their first missionary journey. They had crossed over Cyprus and then sailed to Perga on the coast of Asia Minor, before making the strenuous mountain journey to Pisidian Antioch, which was in the region known as Galatia. And on the Jewish Sabbath they had visited the local synagogue to meet with the Jewish community there, and Paul used the invitation to speak as an opportunity to proclaim a wholehearted gospel message, rich in Old Testament references but centred on the work of Christ.

But the reaction was mixed to say the least. Some became Christians, for Paul and Barnabas 'talked with them and urged them to continue in the grace of God' (Acts 13:43).

And the next Sabbath it would appear that word had got round the whole city because of the amazing numbers of Gentiles who joined with the Jews to hear what Paul had to say. And though there were many conversions again, jealousy was so stirred up that Paul and Barnabas had to move on from the city.

Luke includes a phrase in this account to describe what is happening when opposition arises and Paul and Barnabas announce they will focus upon Gentile evangelism. In verse 48: 'When the Gentiles heard this, they were glad and honoured the word of the Lord; and all who were appointed for eternal life believed'.

Now the Greek word that Luke uses here is '*tasso*', which means to ordain or decree. Sometimes it is used with the meaning of assigning someone to a particular group, and sometimes the word has been used with the idea of someone who has been inscribed or enrolled in a particular book.

In fact Luke uses this particular word three other times in Acts:

> This brought Paul and Barnabas into sharp dispute and debate with them. So Paul and Barnabas were **appointed**, along with some other believers, to go up to Jerusalem to see the apostles and elders about this question (15:2).

> "What shall I do, Lord?" I asked. "Get up," the Lord said, "and go into Damascus. There you will be told all that you have been **assigned** to do" (22:10).

> They **arranged** to meet Paul on a certain day, and came in even larger numbers to the place where he was staying (28:23).

What Luke seems to be accepting as perfectly normal is that doctrine that we know as election, or predestination. Wayne Grudem summarises election like this: 'Election is an act of God before creation in which he chooses some people to be saved, not on account of any foreseen merit in them, but only because of his sovereign good pleasure'.[21]

Now for various reasons this offends some people. Yet it is hard to deny that this is what the Bible teaches in various places. Because this is a vital matter, let me take you through some of these references:

And this is the will of him who sent me, that I shall lose none of all that he has given me, but raise them up at the last day (John 6:39).

For he chose us in him before the creation of the world to be holy and blameless in his sight. In love he predestined us to be adopted as his sons through Jesus Christ, in accordance with his pleasure and will (Eph. 1:4-5).

In him we were also chosen, having been predestined according to the plan of him who works out everything in conformity with the purpose of his will, in order that we, who were the first to hope in Christ, might be for the praise of his glory (Eph. 1:11-12).

For we know, brothers and sisters loved by God, that he has chosen you, because our gospel came to you not simply with words, but also with power, with the Holy Spirit and with deep conviction (1 Thess. 1:4-5).

But we ought always to thank God for you, brothers and sisters loved by the Lord, because from the beginning God chose you to be saved through the sanctifying work of the Spirit and through belief in the truth (2 Thess. 2:13).

… God, who has saved us and called us to a holy life— not because of anything we have done but because of his own purpose and grace. This grace was given us in Christ Jesus before the beginning of time (2 Tim.1:9).

Peter, an apostle of Jesus Christ, To God's elect (1 Pet. 1:1).

But you are a chosen people, a royal priesthood, a holy nation, a people belonging to God (1 Pet. 2:9).

The inhabitants of the earth whose names have not been written in the book of life from the creation of the world will be astonished when they see the beast (Rev. 17:8).

Indeed, this is recognised within the 39 Articles of the Church of England.

Article 17 says this:

Predestination to life is the everlasting purpose of God, whereby (before the foundations of the world were laid) he hath constantly decreed by his counsel secret to us, to deliver from curse and damnation those whom he hath chosen in Christ out of mankind, and to bring them by Christ to everlasting salvation, as vessels made to honour.

But let me pick up on two of the commonest objections that are raised to this teaching.

The first suggests that God chose those whom he saw would respond to him by faith. And in this way they try to reconcile God's electing call with their understanding of man's free will.

And the passage that is used to make this point is Romans 8:28-30:

And we know that in all things God works for the good of those who love him, who have been called according to his purpose. For those God foreknew he also predestined to be conformed to the likeness of his Son, that he might be the firstborn among many brothers and sisters. And those he predestined, he also called; those he called, he also justified; those he justified, he also glorified.

And the argument is that God looked into the future, saw who would choose him, and so predestined them to be his children. But the trouble is, this falls down in a number of ways.

a) God's foreknowledge, spoken of in Romans 8, does not mean foreknowledge of what people would do (there is no reference to that): rather it is an expression used in the Bible to describe God's knowledge of real people whom he thought of in a saving relationship to himself before they ever drew breath.

b) Such an understanding of foreknowledge means that salvation is dependent upon some merit or choice of our own. We chose God therefore he chose us. Our faith becomes the reason God chooses us. But the Bible clearly speaks of salvation as being by grace alone, not by works. It says that even our saving faith was given us by God.

c) Such an understanding of foreknowledge is, in effect, deeply fatalistic. It teaches that people are bound to make certain choices that nothing can change – that's why they argue God is able to elect them, because he is certain that they will not change. But this smacks of an impersonal fate, whereas the Bible teaches that a loving, personal God sovereignly rules his creation in an active and intimate manner.

But the second major objection that is often raised to the Bible's teaching on election, and will be expressed by readers of this book, is that it kills evangelism. If certain people are going to be saved and that is already determined by God and nothing can stop his purposes, then why bother preaching the gospel, praying for the lost, reaching out in acts of love and mercy?

I love the answer that Whitefield gave to Wesley:

O dear Sir, what kind of reasoning – or rather sophistry – is this! Hath not God, who hath appointed salvation for a certain number, appointed also the preaching of the word as a means to bring them to it? Does anyone hold election in any other sense? And if so, how is preaching needless to them that are elected, when the gospel is designated by God himself to be the power of God unto their eternal salvation? And since we know not who are elect and who reprobate, we are to preach promiscuously to all.[22]

This brings us to the heart of the paradox. Though salvation is all of God's electing grace, it must be accompanied by the proclamation of that gospel. We must be careful that it is not flawed human logic that is trusted in here; rather, we need to see what the Bible itself teaches. And in this passage where Luke speaks of God having appointing people to salvation, he also records the passionate preaching and warning of Paul himself.

Listen to Paul's plea at the end of his first sermon:

Therefore, my brothers and sisters, I want you to know that through Jesus the forgiveness of sins is proclaimed to you. Through him everyone who believes is justified from everything you could not be justified from by the law of Moses. Take care that what the prophets have said does not happen to you: "Look, you scoffers, wonder and perish, for I am going to do something in your days that you would never believe, even if someone told you" (Acts 13:38-41).

And then his answer to the rioting Jews:

Then Paul and Barnabas answered them boldly: "We had to speak the word of God to you first. Since you reject it and do not consider yourselves worthy of eternal life, we now turn to the Gentiles" (Acts 13:46).

So here is the biblical paradox that we must at all times maintain. Chosen yet accountable.

No one in hell will ever say they are there because it is God's fault; each will be there because of their own sin, guilt, failure and rejection. Each sinner is accountable before God. God's electing purposes are no excuse for the sinner's lack of response.

And, conversely, everyone in heaven will acknowledge they are there entirely because of God's mercy and love and grace. They will acknowledge to his eternal praise and honour that salvation is from God from start to finish. It is all of his grace; it is nothing of our choosing.

Think what this wonderful truth of God's electing grace means to each Christian.

a) It humbles me before God. It exposes my utter lostness and reveals his awesome power. Romans 9:14-16 says:

> What then shall we say? Is God unjust? Not at all! For he says to Moses, "I will have mercy on whom I have mercy, and I will have compassion on whom I have compassion". It does not, therefore, depend on man's desire or effort, but on God's mercy.

b) It assures me of my future salvation. God has chosen me so I can never be lost.

> And we know that in all things God works for the good of those who love him, who have been called according to his purpose. For those God foreknew he also predestined to be conformed to the likeness of his Son, that he might be the firstborn among many brothers and sisters. And those he predestined, he also called; those he called, he also justified; those he justified, he also glorified. What, then, shall we say in response to this? If God is for us, who can be against us? ... For I am convinced that neither death nor life, neither angels nor demons, neither the present nor the future, nor any powers, neither height nor depth, nor anything else in all creation, will be able to separate us from the love of God that is in Christ Jesus our Lord (Rom. 8:28-31, 38-39).

c) It fills me with praise and wonder. As the implications of this truth sink in, I can do nothing else but praise and worship the living God.

> In love he predestined us to be adopted as his children through Jesus Christ, in accordance with his pleasure

and will – to the praise of his glorious grace. In him we were also chosen, having been predestined according to the plan of him who works out everything in conformity with the purpose of his will, in order that we, who were the first to hope in Christ, might be for the praise of his glory (Eph. 1:5-6, 11-12).

d) It helps me deal with suffering. When I have grasped the full extent of God's sovereign purposes, I can rest in him all the more fully when trouble and difficulty and disappointment comes. The rock on which I rest is his unfailing purposes for me and promises to me.

e) It encourages me in evangelism. If I was called to be an evangelist I don't know I'd be able to cope if I thought that the results were down to me and my gifts of persuasion. How could I cope every time I declare the gospel and people walk away from Christ, not accepting his claims, and realised it was my fault? Whereas when I know that salvation is all of God, that he has his people, that he is calling his elect, that he is building his church, that he will give the gifts necessary to complete the task – I am ready to endure anything for the sake of God's elect. 2 Timothy 2:8-10 says

> Remember Jesus Christ, raised from the dead, descended from David. This is my gospel, for which I am suffering even to the point of being chained like a criminal. But God's Word is not chained. Therefore I endure everything for the sake of the elect, that they too may obtain the salvation that is in Christ Jesus, with eternal glory.

Because the gospel is God's story that he will use to open the eyes of the spiritually blind, I can have absolute confidence in it. I don't need to dilute it or add to it. I don't need to pep it up with gadgets or gizmos, smoke machines or orchestras. I don't need to try and make it more relevant because it is the most up to date and needed message going. I just need to know it, feel it, live it and speak it to the people that God sovereignly brings my way.

There is no doubt much more that could and should be said about this subject. Let me give John Stott the final word here:

> Wherever we look in Scripture we see this antinomy [a logical contradiction which cannot be resolved]: divine sovereignty and human responsibility, universal offer or electing purpose, the all and the some, the cannot and the will not. The right response to this phenomenon is neither to seek a superficial harmonisation nor to declare that Jesus and Paul contradicted themselves, but to affirm both parts of the antinomy as true, while humbly confessing that at present our little minds are unable to resolve it.[23]

Chapter Thirteen

Intentionality

Our home in inner-city Bristol was separated from the church building by a railway line. There were three points at which I could cross: one over a bridge or two through separate tunnels under that same track. There's little difference in the time it takes to walk, so what determines the route? The weather? Desire for variety? No – my wife and I decided we'd walk the same route every time for the sake of the gospel. We wanted to become familiar to traders and residents along that route, with the longing that we might get to know them and be able to speak of Jesus in our interactions. Our route was intentional.

Then there was a Facebook group specific to the postal code where we lived. I joined up, not only so I might get to hear of what was going on in our locality, but so I could post comments pointing to special services at our church. And then one day I noticed an advert posted on the Facebook group about a book club that meets above the main 'hub' pub. Realising I could make most of the evenings when it met, I went along, read the books and joined in the discussion, inevitably having my own 'Christian world-view' opinions. Intentionality.

Because if there's one criticism that could be levelled against the ideas contained in this book it's this – 'You're giving Christians an excuse to do nothing evangelistically. You're justifying passivity. It's a coward's charter'.

But that's to misunderstand what we're suggesting. The biblical expectation is that we live the whole of life under the

Lordship of Jesus Christ. And that means that not only will we have a deep understanding of and appreciation for the saving work of Christ, but we'll also be profoundly affected by the reality of God's wrath against sin and the eternal fate of those who die without coming to a saving faith in Christ's finished work. So we'll always be on the lookout for ways to connect with friends and family, colleagues and neighbours. How could it be otherwise?

You see, gospel intentionality should extend to every area of life. In the workplace thought will be given to how I spend my coffee-breaks and lunch hours. Where's the best place to meet with my colleagues and get to know them better? Maybe it will be the pub or the work canteen, maybe it means bringing a packed lunch to eat with that person you're concerned for; maybe it means sharing a lift in a car or travelling by public transport. The constant motivation is what enables me to best connect for gospel purposes. Sometimes it might be good to open your Bible and read it at work; on other occasions that might not be the wisest choice. Gospel intentionality must shape our actions.

Perhaps you don't go out to paid work and are based in the home. How can you use that time best to show and share Christ? There might be neighbours who would value a visit or would appreciate some shopping; there might be jobs you can do for others where they live; a community group might meet nearby to talk over local issues; refugees might have relocated near you and require language help and advocacy. The possibilities are endless.

Such intentionality doesn't just happen. It requires careful thought and should result in specific actions. All too often our diaries shape and control us. We feel out of control or just trapped in the 'same old, same old'. Whereas we're the ones who should be shaping our agendas with deliberate and careful gospel intentionality, rather than let our sovereignly ordained lives drift along without a moment's thought for how they might be used for King Jesus.

Chapter Fourteen

Responding wisely

'Be wise in the way you act towards outsiders; make the most of every opportunity. Let your conversation be always full of grace, seasoned with salt, so that you may know how to answer everyone' (Col. 4:5-6).

What can make our conversations salty? How should we respond when opportunities arise? Let me suggest a few principles that emerge from the Apostle Paul's practice.

Firstly, we must start from where people are – rather than assume they're familiar with biblical concepts and ideas. As we'll discuss later, it's quite possible that their whole world-view sees things completely differently to you. Maybe you've been a Christian for a long time and instinctively you think in categories defined by your faith. So you talk about sin and the Bible and the sacrifice of Jesus on the cross and assume your friend will immediately understand the words and terms you are using. But it is quite possible – indeed likely – that their whole world-view has been shaped by a variety of other influences that may have been quite 'anti-Christian' in their origin. If that's the case, there's little point in talking to them about the fact that they have 'fallen short of the glory of God' when they have no comprehension of what those terms mean. We need to start further back. We need to understand those we're chatting with as well as the message that we're sharing.

I was profoundly helped and affected by reading a book by Roy Joslin called *Urban Harvest* back in the 1980s. It opened my eyes to the different approaches that Paul adopted for sharing the gospel in Pisidian Antioch and Lystra (Acts 13, 14). In Pisidian Antioch Paul was addressing Jews and God-fearing Gentiles within the context of a synagogue gathering. He identifies as a Jew and bases his argument upon the commonly acknowledged authority of God's Word. He outlines Jewish history and points to Jesus the Messiah who fulfilled the Messianic promises.

Whereas when we come to Lystra we discover an entirely different community. This is a farming community made up of a largely uneducated population who seemed to be ignorant of Greek culture and who speak their own language ('Lycaonian' Acts 14:11). Does Paul get out his old sermon notes from Pisidian Antioch and preach the same message? Not at all. The Lycaonians would not have understood. In fact, Paul makes no reference at all to Scripture, although all that he says is biblical. Instead, Paul appeals to the universal witness of creation, something he is to later write about to the church in Rome (Rom. 1:19-20). Here is something those in Lystra could relate to – simple, uncomplicated and visually illustrated, free from abstract Greek thought.

And in the same way we need to understand, as far as we can, where our friend is coming from and what they can relate to. The core gospel message never changes, but it's not a one-size-fits-all presentation. This only goes to underline what we have been saying previously, that the good news about Jesus is best presented in the context of relationships of trust and friendship, where we understand the person we're sharing with and know how to connect with their own life experience and categories.

And then, secondly (and closely related to the first point), is that we must speak their language. What I mean by that is there's no point using words that have no meaning to our listeners. When I'm with biblically literate believers I'm really happy to talk and sing about being washed in the blood of the lamb. It's precious and richly biblical language but my friend next door wouldn't have a clue what I was talking about. In fact, I would be rising up his 'weirdo' meter very quickly, and in danger of losing his friendship. Instead, I want to use phrases and descriptions that are accessible to him.

I imagine that many who read this book (and have got this far!) have received some form of academic or professional training, and therefore we're accustomed to and have been trained in grappling with complex language that may well be highly conceptual. But not everyone has – not necessarily because of ability but because of experience. Therefore the language we use must be appropriate to our hearer. Jesus, the master communicator, used language full of 'concrete' thought forms as opposed to abstract expressions, whereas Paul, in defining and defending the gospel message, found the more conceptual Greek language a better vehicle for his purposes. One is not better than the other. We must never play off the gospels against the letters. But what we are saying is that we need to exercise discernment and wisdom to ensure that we communicate as clearly as we can with the listener before us. We need to remember that most thinking in Western culture is shaped by television (where even for a news journalist the average length of a report is 18 seconds), or Twitter (messages now confined to 280 characters) or Facebook (where the optimal length of a status update is said to be 40 characters).

Then thirdly, we need to identify with our hearers. What points of contact can we establish? What do we have in common? Does our friend think we can enter into what they are going through? Or do we come over as aliens from another planet trying to enforce our ideas upon them?

Paul was the master at connecting with his hearers whatever the situation. In Pisidian Antioch and Ephesus he connects as a Jew; in Athens he connects through what he had seen whilst walking around the city; before the rioting crowd in Jerusalem he tells them of his religious training; and in writing to the Corinthians he argues for appropriate flexibility so that we might effectively communicate with our hearers (1 Cor. 9:19-23).

The reality is that you and I will share many experiences with others who live in this broken and fallen world: disappointments and regrets, broken hearts and failing health, miscarriages and bereavements; the list goes on. And it's in the course of a friendship that we'll be able to discover where we connect, and what it might be that will enable our friends to understand what we're trying to say.

Fourthly, when sharing with our friends we should use appropriate illustrations and expressions. Tim Keller encourages us to subvert their way of thinking by using illustrations drawn from their own cultural authorities. Of course, this is what Paul did before the Areopagus in Athens – he quotes two of their own poets, Epimenides and Aratus. And for us the poets of our age are those whose music is followed. Any cursory viewing of the Glastonbury music festival will show tens of thousands singing out words they had memorised from their favourite artist, and whilst many of these lyrics are anodyne or worse, there are some that reflect the angst, confusion and despair of the modern age. Just one example out of many would be Taylor Swift's song '22':

> We're happy free confused and lonely at the same time
> It's miserable and magical oh yeah
> Tonight's the night when we forget about the deadlines, it's time uh oh
> I don't know about you but I'm feeling 22
> Everything will be alright, if you keep me next to you.

Let me give you two examples of what has been written or said by well-respected academics and thinkers which can be used to expose the inconsistency and assumptions of their own clan. The philosopher Thomas Nagel, back in 1997, wrote this in his book *The Last Word*:

I want atheism to be true and am made uneasy by the fact that some of the most intelligent and well-informed people I know are religious believers. It isn't just that I don't believe in God and, naturally, hope that I'm right in my belief. It's that I hope there is no God! I don't want there to be a God; I don't want the universe to be like that.[24]

The flawed but brilliant American writer and university professor David Foster Wallace said this at a commencement address in 2005, three years before he hanged himself:

A huge percentage of the stuff that I tend to be automatically certain of is, it turns out, totally wrong and deluded. Here's one example of the utter wrongness of something I tend to be automatically sure of: Everything in my own immediate experience supports my deep belief that I am the absolute centre of the universe, the realest, most vivid and important person in existence. We rarely talk about this sort of natural, basic self-centeredness, because it's so socially repulsive, but it's pretty much the same for all of us, deep down. It is our default setting, hardwired into our boards at birth.

And if we keep our eyes and ears open there are numerous contemporary illustrations that will help us make our communication as clear and effective as we can. The Christian blogosphere will often pick up such gems, and it's a good idea to keep up to date with one or two trusted bloggers who might point us in the right direction.

But often we don't even need to go that far. News stories of celebrities and sporting heroes, of events both tragic and glorious, give us a deep pool to swim in for our illustrations. There may be some wisdom in knowing in outline (if not watching every episode) dramas that are shaping conversations at work or outside the school. What point are they making? What questions are they raising? And how does your distinctive viewpoint as a believer contribute to the discussions they provoke?

We should not be surprised that with all the wonders of common grace and all the pain and turmoil of living in our fallen world there are numerous ways the gospel can intersect with and illustrate the issues facing our friends. We just need to be ready.

Fifthly, we should be delighted and able to speak of what actually happened to us when we became Christians and speak of the effect it had upon us. We should show that this is earthed in everyday reality. At times this is where our language can again let us down. We need to go beyond the cliché. To say that I was 'born again' is both glorious and confusing. It needs careful unpacking. Or to say that 'I asked Jesus into my heart' suffers from the same problems. It's probably best to find other ways to explain what God has done in your life. Of course, this means you not only need to be self-aware, you also need to be theologically acute, conscious of what God has actually done in giving you new life, and how the death and resurrection of Christ is central in your story. You don't need a theology degree to do this but you should be sufficiently informed about the greatest thing that's happened in your experience. After all, you know how you got here biologically, so shouldn't you have the same awareness of what happened spiritually? The danger can be that our laziness and ignorance will allow us to fall back upon that incomprehensible 'evangelical speak' rather than having a sufficient grasp of our salvation to enable us to shape our communication naturally for the hearer before us.

We need to remember that we live in an age when telling your own story is far more acceptable than it may have been a generation or two ago. Because we live in a multi-ethnic, multi-cultural society we are more ready to listen to one another's experiences. Aneurin Bevan, the Welsh Labour politician, once said 'This is my truth, now tell me yours', which in turn became the title for the Manic Street Preachers 1998 album and summed up the way society was changing. In an age when society considers each truth as valid as another, however contradictory, we should use this opening and let our 'truths' be known, confident that a sovereign God can and will vindicate the message of grace.

It's probably worth thinking through your unique salvation story and working out how you could communicate it with someone who asks. See if you can get it down to under five minutes in a cliché-free zone. And maybe ask a Christian friend to critique what you have prepared. It's amazing the blind spots we can develop.

Are you ready?

Chapter Fifteen

Anticipating the questions

As we have seen, both Paul and Peter expect that every believer should be ready to respond to the questions that will come their way. But what are these questions likely to be, and can we prepare ourselves by considering the issues in advance? How foolish not to be ready when some advance thinking and planning might open an opportunity to share my faith.

Firstly, identifying the main issues.

As far as I can see it, these come in three areas – the emotional, the intellectual and the social.

In the emotional area we are not at all surprised to discover that questions to do with suffering are number one on our list. We live in a broken and fallen world and are all subject to pain, disease and death and our innate, God-shaped sense of justice cries out against the seeming contradiction of a sovereign and loving God allowing these things to happen.

In a famous interview on Irish television, Stephen Fry, the much-loved actor and raconteur, was asked by Gabriel Bryne 'Suppose it's all true, and you walk up to the pearly gates, and are confronted by God what will Stephen Fry say to him, her, or it?' He replied:

'I'd say, "Bone cancer in children? What's that about? How dare you? How dare you create a world to which

there is such misery that is not our fault. It's not right,
it's utterly, utterly evil".

Why should I respect a capricious, mean-minded, stupid
God who creates a world that is so full of injustice and
pain. That's what I would say'.

The novelist Somerset Maugham wrote something similar.
'I'm glad I don't believe in God. When I look at the misery
of the world and its bitterness I think that no belief can be
more ignoble'.[25]

And in my (ageing) record collection I have an Elton John
record that contains the lyrics:

'If there's a God in heaven
What's he waiting for
If He can't hear the children
Then he must see the war
But it seems to me
That he leads his lambs
To the slaughter house
And not the promised land'

These quotes seem to sum up the anger and hostility that many
feel towards God when faced with the issue of suffering. And
it would be foolish of Christians in the extreme to dismiss the
deep pain and harrowing experiences that many have been
through that have scarred their lives. This is no place for quick,
easy, simplistic answers. There are none. So often in situations
like this, when faced with deeply personal questions demanding
to know 'why', the Christian must gently and honestly confess
they do not know. As we'll see in the next section so often the
best and most loving thing to do is to get our friend to tell us
more about the situation that has prompted that question.

But where some answers are required then I think we need
to explore how incredibly holy and loving God is and how
deeply vile and abhorrent our sin really is. We can carefully

illustrate from the lives of some who have suffered deeply and reflected upon it (C.S. Lewis and Helmut Thielicke come to mind). We can speak about the choices that people freely make and the consequences that flow from them. And above all we can point to the suffering of the cross and the glorious hope of heaven.

In one paragraph I can only faintly point in directions that would take up volumes of more considered work, but at least here are some signposts to guide us in our thinking. Further reading and careful thought is certainly required.

The intellectual questions that may arise in the course of conversation are rarely (in my experience) original to the questioner. Often they have been picked up second hand from the opinions expressed and popularised by others. It's not to say that they're not good and genuine questions, but rather they're being used as a form of defence against the claims of Christ and may be countered more directly than issues that have arisen from the heart.

The usual suspects here are to do with evidence for the existence of God, the supposed contradictions that 'litter' the Bible and issues relating to science and evolution. Once again let me say that it's not my job here to provide the definitive answers to these objections – they are well dealt with in other specialist works – but rather to encourage you to research, prepare and anticipate – to be 'ready'.

I well remember a sixth-form discussion where a teacher quickly dealt with the claims of the Christian faith by declaring that 'we all know the Bible is full of contradictions'. When I asked him to give me one or two illustrations of such, he quickly became flustered, defensive and mute. This is not to say that there aren't some issues that at first glance may appear to be contradictory, but further research and deeper biblical knowledge can usually resolve these within a few minutes. Remember – these are generally the fig-leaf questions that are there to cover over the enquirer's preconceptions and prejudices.

I'm not a scientist so questions to do with this area are harder for me to deal with if I am talking to a friend who has greater scientific knowledge. So I was very heartened to hear Professor John Lennox tell us that the big question we need to keep coming back to is that of origins. Where did it all start? What was before the 'big bang', if indeed that was how it all started? If my friend is unable to answer that most basic and essential of questions then we hardly need spend hours talking about some of the finer details of the debate.

The third category of question is what I've entitled the 'social' dimension. These are the questions that reflect the assumptions of living in a pluralist society, where there is a strong reaction to Christianity's claims and teachings. Some of the most common objections I've been hearing are to do with the claims that the Christian faith is homophobic or transphobic, or to do with the exclusive claims that Christ is the only way – 'What about other religions?'

These are some of the hardest objections to deal with. In our questioner's mind it is entirely unthinkable that the Christian faith should have a place within our secular, pluralist society. They cannot possibly understand how Christians could be so 'narrow' and 'bigoted'. Indeed the pressure to bring Christian teaching 'up to date' and make it 'relevant' is so great that many denominations and individuals have caved in under the weight. Sadly the response of many in society has become so aggressive and censorious that it can be very hard to have any meaningful and open discussion.

Of course there are glorious answers to do with these issues and believers have written so helpfully to describe the true story of human flourishing under God's magnificent grace, and many have gently exposed the gaping contradictions within the prevailing world-view. (For example, Rebecca McLaughlin has written most helpfully on these issues. See the bibliography.) But the question remains as to whether they will get a hearing. That's why it is vital that all God's children live all of their lives reflecting the grace and beauty of Jesus in all they do.

Christians love lesbian, gay, bi-sexual, transgender and queer folk. They will speak graciously and act lovingly. They will use every opportunity to bless all people who come within their orbit. They will show mercy and engage in acts that will bless and help all they meet. And it is as the love of Christ is worked out in everyday situations that little by little, one by one, the prejudices and stereotypes are demolished and opportunities arise to share the best story of all.

We've tried to identify the main issues and broken them down into three areas – the emotional, the intellectual and the social. But then secondly, we should be ready to answer questions with questions.

We should do this because it's what Jesus did. Martin Copenhaver suggests that in the New Testament it's recorded that Jesus asked 307 questions.[26] Of course (as we will later see) this was such a natural thing to do within an Honour / Shame culture, where unnecessary confrontation would be deemed counterproductive. But that does not detract from its value for us.

We should also do this because it's a highly relational thing to do. We move beyond firing bullets at the other person from a distance to getting to know them better. As we've suggested, so many of the questions that we're asked arise out of the questioner's experience, and it's as we enter into their world that we can begin to grasp better what are the real issues that may lie behind the initial enquiry. Furthermore, questions reveal that we are genuinely concerned for them and don't see them as anonymous gospel fodder who will be satisfied with the generic answer. We really do care about their circumstances and family, their life experiences and their hurts. Questions add colour and depth to the person we're engaging with.

And questions are the ideal vehicle to expose the sometimes muddled thinking that generates the enquiry of our friend. It allows them to think for themselves and own the answers that they come up with. It avoids the confrontational situation that provokes proud people to dig their heels in (which characterises ourselves as well as our questioning friend) and instead honours our friend enough to explore their own thinking and reasoning.

If this resonates with you, you might want to explore further the work done by Randy Newman in this area.[27] It would certainly help you to be ready!

And then finally in this chapter, we need to recognise that it is often very wise to get our questioning friend to Jesus as quickly as possible. After all, he is the ultimate answer to all our life questions and the one who is the focus of the Bible's overarching salvation story. Indeed, when we are dealing with our friend's questions that fall into the emotional or social categories that we mentioned earlier, Jesus is the ideal person to take them to.[28] When it comes to questions of suffering, he is the glorious illustration of how God took suffering and brokenness upon himself and can empathise with us in our pain and distress. The cross, like no other place, speaks of the heights of God's holiness and the depths of his love.

And for the person who feels like an outcast or outsider, the story of Jesus continually shouts of one who came to be the friend of sinners – one who had harsher words for the legalistic religious professional than for the seeking soul, one who welcomed the riff-raff of society and melded them together as his disciples. Well-shaped arguments are fine, rigorous logic has its place, propositions are necessary – but it is Jesus who towers majestically above them all in drawing seeking sinners to himself. Be ready to point them to him.

Chapter Sixteen

Telling the better story

In the previous two chapters we've been considering some of the ways we can respond to the questions of our friends. We've touched upon 'apologetics' – the answers we can give and the areas we can explore by way of defending and clarifying the Christian gospel. But as we also noted, our Western society is changing so rapidly that an approach based on reason and logic alone can appear overly authoritarian and controlling and be dismissed without a hearing.

This, of course, is not to say that we shouldn't be conversant with ways to address the objections that others may raise, but rather to note that a number of contemporary Christian thinkers have been suggesting other ways we can engage with our friends. Dan Strange, in his book *Making Faith Magnetic,* builds upon the work of J.H. Bavinck and suggests there are five fundamental things for which all human beings are searching – totality, norm, deliverance, destiny and higher power. Dan goes on to show how Jesus fulfils each of these universal longings. His contention is that we have more in common with our non-Christian friends than we might imagine (magnetic points) and that by telling our story and sharing our struggles in these areas we should be better equipped to share Christ.

'We come as those offering answers to questions they are already answering, offering an exchange for religious commitments they already have, and offering a way to mend a relationship with God they are already in'.[29]

Joshua Chatraw adopts a similar approach. In his book *Telling a Better Story* he proposes an 'inside/outside' method. Having sensitively listened to a person's story we become aware how we can connect the gospel message to their lives. Chatraw's five 'magnetic points' are inclusiveness, reason, happiness, being true to yourself, and finding ultimate meaning. He suggests that on the 'inside' we ask ourselves how we connect with the major themes of our friend's story, and whether what they are saying is consistent and liveable. And then on the 'outside' we try to see what our friend's narrative has borrowed from the Christian story, and how our own Christian narrative actually better addresses their observations and experiences.

Now I'm not pretending that this approach is instantly accessible. Some of us are struggling to come to terms with the vast and rapid changes to the way society thinks and we're still playing catch-up in how we can share the gospel message with a society that despises or ignores it. But at its heart, the invitation for us to tell a better story is compelling. We need to subvert the narrative of our age by gently inviting our friends to hear how Jesus answers the very aches that we all wrestle with.

And on the 'sexual' battle-front, where a lot of today's narratives are being formed, Glynn Harrison has written a superb book entitled *A Better Story: God, Sex and Human Flourishing*. It complements perfectly the previously two mentioned books by focusing with clarity and compassion on the radical individualism that is shaping today's view of sex. Once again the diagnosis is to live and tell out the better story that we have in Christ.

And it may be that in engaging with these three helpful books we will be 'ready' to better give an answer for the hope we have.

Chapter Seventeen

Understanding the questioner

Context is everything. We find that when looking at Bible passages. And we find that when talking to others. Where are they 'coming from'? What life experiences have shaped them? What influences have governed their thinking? In the previous chapters we have recognised that the use of wise questions is an essential diagnostic tool if we are to respond in gracious and appropriate ways. But what if my friend works on a different 'operating system'? What if their default way of seeing the world is 'Apple' when mine is 'Windows'? Can I assume that what comes out of my mouth is processed accurately and can be 'run' in their thinking?

I'd always thought that clear communication was all that was needed in articulating gospel truths. I'd assumed that the categories of thought I employed were the same for everyone. It wasn't until trying to share the gospel with our lovely Muslim neighbours that I realised our words were missing each other. I would use an expression such as 'sin' and discovered that it didn't connect at all with them. They would interpret my words in ways that I didn't intend. It was as if there were these two different operating systems that couldn't process the data from one to the other.

Well, I came to understand that these operating systems were actually our 'cultural paradigms' – ways of thinking, living, responding and acting – that have been hardwired into us from our upbringing. And, horror of horrors, I discovered that my cultural paradigm ('innocence / guilt') was not shared by the majority of the globe's inhabitants, nor was it the controlling paradigm for the vast majority of Bible writers. It was a humbling moment to be reminded (again) that I was not at the central resting point of the pendulum's arc. I was an outsider who needed to re-evaluate how I processed and passed on information and experience.

I understood this better when I reflected on my reactions to the music being played in a small church in northern Pakistan. To my ear it sounded unnatural and strange; I didn't appreciate the rhythms and musical progression, it didn't have harmonies my ears rejoiced in.

Why? Because I'd grown up listening to music based upon the diatonic scale, where the progression is based upon using a chain of six perfect fifths, making up twelve notes per octave. And I'd appreciate the genius of a Mozart or a Springsteen based on that inherited, inbuilt sense.

But not everyone hears it that way. They've been brought up differently, and classical Asian music is largely based upon a pentatonic scale which is made up of five notes. What we instinctively appreciate as being great music doesn't instinctively connect with those who inherited and were brought up with a classical Asian music tradition. So we both struggle to communicate with each other about music because we come from such differing backgrounds. One genre of music isn't better than the other, it's just different, although my 'me-centrism' assumes that what I hear and appreciate is what everyone will hear and appreciate.

That's how it is with the gospel as we seek to communicate with those who come from a different cultural paradigm. We assume that they 'get' the points we are trying to make, when actually what they're hearing is quite different to the point we're making.

That's why there's been a recent spurt of missional activity in trying to understand and engage with these different cultural paradigms. And this will increase over the next decade as this insight gains ground. And if we're to be ready to speak of Jesus in our increasingly cross-cultural communities we cannot afford to go on ignoring the dynamics that are in play today. We need to understand each one of those we communicate with and check to see if we are speaking the same 'language'. Sadly, some evangelism I've witnessed seems to be the equivalent of shouting at speakers of other languages believing that the louder the noise, the more likely it is they'll understand.

This is not the place to give a thorough explanation of the paradigms we need to be aware of. The literature is growing and an excellent website (www.HonorShame.com) provides a wealth of resources, but allow me to make some very general observations.

There are three major cultural paradigms. There's the 'Guilt / Innocence' culture, which is mainly represented within North America, Europe, Australia and New Zealand. There's the 'Honour / Shame' culture, mainly represented within the Majority World, and then there's the 'Power / Fear' culture that still can be seen in parts of Africa. What we need to remember is that these do not contain easily identifiable boundaries. It would be unusual to find one person who represented the 'pure' nature of one exclusive group. Each of these cultural paradigms bleed into one another and to varying degrees are found present in most of us.

So it's not so much Fig. 1:

As it is Fig. 2:

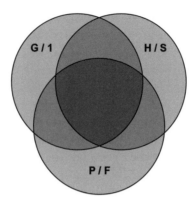

Each one reading this book will be somewhere on this diagram. There is no neutral place. There is nowhere for one to adopt a position of pure objectivity.

The task for us now is to try and understand in the broadest terms how these different paradigms operate and regard each other. We'll focus on the two dominating paradigms – the Innocence / Guilt paradigm (IG) and the Honour / Shame paradigm (HS). The following list will give some idea of the cultural values imbedded within each and how one culture views the attitudes of the other.

When it comes to relationships, IG places a strong emphasis upon equality which HS would regard as disrespectful, whereas HS places a strong emphasis upon hierarchy which IG would regard as oppressive.

With time, IG tends to be task-focused which HS would regard as unkind, whereas HS places the emphasis upon the interpersonal event focus which to the IG seems to be inconsiderate.

With speech, IG highly regards truth which to HS might consider rude, whereas HS places the emphasis upon harmony which to the IG seems to be dishonest.

With money, IG places a high value on independence which HS might regard as stingy, whereas HS puts an emphasis upon patronage which seems corrupt to IG.

With food, IG seems to place importance upon efficiency which HS would regard as neglectful, whereas HS places the emphasis upon hospitality which to IG can seem ostentatious.

Finally, in the realm of ethics IG is built upon a guilt-based culture which to HS can come over as shameless, whereas HS culture is shame-based which to IG appears lawless.

Confused? Let me illustrate it in another way using Brook Peterson's five basic cultural scales and illustrate how an IG culture sits on the other side to positions taken by an HS culture.[30]

(Brooks Peterson's five basic culture scales)

For example, we come across an action of David's that doesn't make much sense to those of us high on the IG scale of equality, but which makes perfect sense to those within an HS culture of hierarchy.

> David said to his men, "The LORD forbid that I should do this thing to my lord, the LORD's anointed, or lift my hand against him, for he is the anointed of the LORD. With these words David rebuked his men and did not allow them to attack Saul. And Saul left the cave and went his way'(1 Sam. 24:6-7).

When you (from within an IG culture) visit your friend (who's also from within an IG culture) it probably seems the most natural thing to help wash up the dishes after an evening meal. In fact, it would be a positively 'good' thing to do. But if you are visiting a friend who's from within an HS culture and you go to help with the dishes, that might be regarded as an insult, for you are violating the hierarchy of that home.

Or let's take the polarities between the direct approach of someone from an IG culture as compared to the person within the HS culture who is far more comfortable with indirect communication. Notice how Jesus responds to confrontation.

'And a man was there with a withered hand. And they asked him, "Is it lawful to heal on the Sabbath?"—so that they might accuse him. He said to them, "Which one of you who has a sheep, if it falls into a pit on the Sabbath, will not take hold of it and lift it out? Of how much more value is a man than a sheep! So it is lawful to do good on the Sabbath"' (Matt. 12:10-12 ESV).

He answers with a question. He avoids direct confrontation. So when we have the opportunity to respond to our friend from an HS culture we need to slow down and be generous with our time. Indirect communication takes longer and should be a far gentler process than the efficient, logic driven communication style of those from within the IG culture. You've probably noticed that the ability to tell stories and parables can be an invaluable tool when communicating in this way.

Or what about the contrast between our very individualistic IG culture and the more group-oriented world of the HS culture? Isaiah gives us an example of how God's personal dealings with him were immediately translated into viewing things through corporate eyes.

And I said: "Woe is me! For I am lost; for I am a man of unclean lips, and I dwell in the midst of a people of unclean lips; ... " (Isa. 6:5 ESV).

Within HS cultures decisions are made much more slowly because of this dynamic, and the place of the church community within the life of the new believer has a far higher place than the IG culture would readily recognise.

The IG culture also places a higher premium on getting a task done than investing in relationships, which would be the HS priority. Mary and Martha represent these extremes.

> … she had a sister called Mary, who sat at the Lord's feet and listened to his teaching. But Martha was distracted with much serving (Luke 10:39-40 ESV).

And what so many of us living within the IG cultural paradigm need to grasp, especially when with a friend from an HS culture, is that spending time with someone is vastly important. These things can't be rushed. That person can't become a project. The relationship must be genuinely developed and treasured in the expectation that the Lord will then provide opportunities for further sharing.

The final axis is that between risk and caution. The IG culture is full of independent risk-takers who then challenge their HS friends to take the radical step of following Jesus Christ as their Lord. But often they can overlook what an enormous step this would mean for their friend. We sometimes look at God's call to Abram as an invitation to go on an exciting 'trip of a lifetime', failing to realise the massive cultural implications this would have had for this childless couple.

> Now the LORD said to Abram, "Go from your country and your kindred and your father's house to the land that I will show you. And I will make of you a great nation, and I will bless you and make your name great, so that you will be a blessing. I will bless those who bless you, and him who dishonours you I will curse, and in you all the families of the earth shall be blessed" (Gen. 12:1-3 ESV).

Now of course the gospel is a call to risk – but, as with Abram, we need to make sure it is accompanied by the assurances of honour and blessing. In this way our HS friend would be encouraged to venture out in faith, dependent upon the faithfulness of our promise-keeping God.

Now there is so much more that could be said upon this subject (SO much more!) and I may have lost some of you along the way in this chapter because we are looking at issues that are rarely, if ever, addressed within the context of being ready to share the good news of Jesus on a personal level. This may have opened your eyes to issues you had never before considered. But as we live in increasingly multi-cultural communities, we each need to see beyond our own cultural horizons for the sake of the gospel.

And lest you think that you won't ever find yourself in such a situation, let me close with some observations from Andy Crouch, who writing in *Christianity Today* in March 2015, suggested that the Innocence / Guilt culture may well be transitioning into a 'Shame' culture and we need to be ready.

> Instead of evolving into a traditional honor–shame culture, large parts of our culture are starting to look something like a postmodern fame–shame culture. Like honor, fame is a public estimation of worth, a powerful currency of status. But fame is bestowed by a broad audience, with only the loosest of bonds to those they acclaim. Some of the most powerful artefacts of contemporary culture—especially youth culture—are preoccupied with the dynamics of fame and shame.
>
> In a fame–shame culture, the only true crime is to publicly exclude—and thus shame—others. Talk of right and wrong is troubling when it is accompanied by seeming indifference to the experience of shame that accompanies judgments of "immorality". So attempts to reiterate traditional Christian sexual ethics fall not on deaf ears, but on ears highly attuned to dynamics of shame and rejection.

The beauty of the gospel is that it acknowledges guilt and shame, covering both with the shame- and guilt-bearing representative Son. What honor–shame cultures are offering to missionaries, our own fame–shame culture may offer as well: a chance, in the depth of both our guilt and our shame, to discover just how completely good that news can be.[31]

Chapter Eighteen

Ready for suffering

A few years ago, I was preaching in Chiang Mai in northern Thailand and used an illustration that was then confirmed by someone in the congregation who told me he was at the event I was referring to. It concerned a daylong rally held to celebrate the 100th anniversary of the coming of missionaries to a certain part of Africa. At the close of a long day of speeches and music, an old, old man stood before the crowd and insisted on speaking. He soon would die, he said, and if he didn't speak, information that he alone possessed would go with him to his grave. He said that when the missionaries arrived, his people thought them strange and their message dubious. The tribal leaders decided to test the missionaries by slowly poisoning them to death. Over a period of months and years, missionary children died one by one. Then, the old man said, 'It was as we watched how they died that we decided we wanted to live as Christians'.

Those who died painful, strange deaths never knew why they were dying or what the impact of their lives and deaths would be. But through it all, they didn't leave. They stayed because they trusted Jesus Christ. They kept going.

And, of course, for the great Christian missionary, the Apostle Paul, his life wasn't one of non-stop travelling from one victorious preaching opportunity to another. In fact, it seems that Paul spent roughly one-quarter of his missionary career in prison. Most cells were dark, especially the inner cells of a prison like the one from which Paul wrote his final letter to Timothy. Unbearable cold, lack of water, cramped quarters and sickening stench from few toilets made sleeping difficult and waking hours miserable. Because of the miserable conditions, many prisoners begged for a speedy death. Others simply committed suicide.

In a setting like this, Paul wrote to Timothy these words:

'Endure hardship with us like a good soldier of Christ Jesus' (2 Tim. 2:3). In other words, 'Keep going, Timothy, keep going'.

And for all we might write about great evangelistic strategies, the hard reality is that God lovingly and wisely often uses the suffering of his children to point to the reality and worth of Christ. For the unbeliever the question about suffering is purely philosophical. They don't actually believe there is a God, so the question of suffering in the world is just a philosophical argument against Christianity. But for the believer, the question of suffering is more than philosophical, it's intensely personal. They know there's a God; they know he's loving and wise, sovereign and powerful – and yet they experience heartache, pain, loss, failure and tears. That's the problem. That's what can be so hard to reconcile. That's what tests faith and reveals Christ like nothing else.

It was an issue addressed by the writer to the Hebrews, especially when he talks about the great heroes of the faith.

> Some faced jeers and flogging, and even chains and imprisonment. They were put to death by stoning; they were sawn in two; they were killed by the sword. They went about in sheepskins and goatskins, destitute, persecuted and ill-treated— the world was not worthy of them (Heb. 11:36-38).

But it wasn't just these greats who endured such suffering. The writer goes on to speak of Jesus himself and what he went through:

> Jesus, the pioneer and perfecter of faith. For the joy that was set before him he endured the cross, scorning its shame, and sat down at the right hand of the throne of God. Consider him who endured such opposition from sinners (Heb. 12:2-3a).

We can scarcely get our heads around what it cost Jesus to die in the place of sinners. The mocking and abuse, the physical agony, the terrible shame, the weight of infinite wrath, the hell of separation.

And then the writer begins to focus upon the Hebrew Christians themselves. They're going through trials and as a result they're beginning to 'grow weary and lose heart' (12:3). Their arms are growing feeble, their knees are growing weak (12:12, 13). But by placing their suffering alongside the suffering of Old Testament saints and supremely alongside Jesus Christ it's as if the writer is saying to them 'This stuff happens. There's pain; there's pressure. And that's normal in the Christian life'.

Indeed, when speaking to his disciples Jesus makes plain the connection between suffering for him and making him known. 'You will be handed over to the local councils and flogged in the synagogues. On account of me you will stand before governors and kings as witnesses to them' (Mark 13:9).

Tony Reinke puts it like this:

> To suffer for the name of Christ is a two-sided equation. The name of Christ is the cause of our added suffering, but the name of Christ also becomes the purpose of our suffering. As cause, we can expect to suffer for the name of Christ. As purpose, we can expect to suffer, so that in our suffering we might testify to the name of Christ.[32]

And Ajith Fernando says 'One of the glaring omissions in modern church growth studies is the key part that suffering has played in the growth of the church'.[33]

Some of us have witnessed this up close and personal in the lives of Christian friends. Neil Todman, a church planting pastor in south Bristol, watched his wife, Elaine, die twenty months after her initial cancer diagnosis at age forty. My wife and I had the privilege of walking this journey with them and sharing both the tears and the laughter. To any who would listen Elaine would repeat – 'God is wise. God is good. God is in control'.

Neil regularly posted updates on Elaine's condition on the church website, using every opportunity to speak of their gospel confidence. It seemed everyone in that community came to hear about Elaine and Jesus. At her funeral the church building was packed to overflowing, with many needing to gather in the hall nearby. And once again folk testified to the startling reality of Jesus being reflected in this dying woman.

And this is a story repeated many times over. Even as I type a dear friend is seriously ill in hospital. He is one of the most godly and gifted church leaders and preachers I have known. Humanly it doesn't make sense that he should suffer as he does. Yet the testimony of God's grace in his life is reaching right from his family, through their community and into areas Mike might never have been able to connect with.

The sobering lesson of this chapter is that Christians should prepare to suffer; for in their suffering the reality and grace of Jesus Christ can shine more clearly than otherwise might have been possible. Are you ready?

Chapter Nineteen

Ian's story

Ian is a 'boomer'. Growing up through the liberating 1960s into the 1970s he began to feel the weight of his upbringing. Being dragged to church by your parents is not cool. It's even worse when your father is the minister. So the natural course was to reject their faith and cause as much trouble as possible. A natural ability with anything mechanical led to an ongoing fascination with bikes, and to working on Harleys in central London. He even managed to crash his bike and fracture his skull while adjusting the fuel feed on the bike he was riding! He gradually slipped into a culture of drink and drugs, often leaving his mother to clear up his trails of vomit.

Marriage and a new career selling antiques did nothing to break the habits that were increasingly taking over his life. It wasn't long before he lost his home and business, and his marriage broke up. He needed to get out of that scene as soon as he could, so with his new girlfriend, Alison, they cut all ties and relocated to France, buying an old farmhouse to renovate. Ian and Alison saw each other as fellow rebels; both trying to escape what they thought were repressive upbringings; both happy to enjoy the drink and drugs that marked out their circle of friends.

For Alison it was a shock to encounter Ian's parents. They weren't what she expected. They still loved and accepted their son, despite the ways he had treated them, and they always provided a welcome open door for them both. Hardly what she expected from Christians. It was a love that made a deep impression upon her life.

Ian and Alison had a son, Louis, in the opening months of 1991, and it felt, at long last, that life was going well and they were happy. They had everything they wanted. They were living the dream. But then in October 1992 Louis went missing. He ran off but not in the direction assumed. Despite frantic calling he couldn't be found anywhere. Search parties were put together to scour the surrounding countryside. And later in the day his twenty-month-old body was found face down in a stream at the bottom of the valley, drowned in a few inches of water.

Their world fell apart. After all they had been through this was too much. Ian blamed God and tore up what he thought was the only Bible in their house. They were heartbroken, shattered, lost in their grief and pain. It was almost impossible to carry on. Ian sank into a deep depression, his sleeplessness filled with memories of what his parents and other Christians had said. He discovered that, unknown to him, Alison had an old copy of The Living Bible. He began to read it, hoping to find a way to deal with the nagging thoughts in his head. What surprised Ian was the honesty of the Bible, revealing the faults and flaws of all but one of the biblical characters. And when he came to Ecclesiastes, he discovered someone who put into words what he was feeling (that life is pointless) and who concluded that only a life lived under God has meaning and purpose. The light began to seep in.

Meanwhile as Alison tried to recover from the tragedy of Louis' death, another event happened that shook her to the core. The roof over a large room next to their kitchen suddenly collapsed. Ian jumped in to rescue some of their furniture while Alison stood by on a short flight of stone steps, looking down into the devastation but terrified that Ian would be crushed by a falling rafter. She found herself crying out to the God she didn't know or believe in but she knew there was nowhere else for her to turn.

It was the turning point for Alison. She didn't want to become a Christian. She struggled believing that Jesus was the only way. She had so many questions. But God's grace broke through.

At virtually the same time Ian's spiritual search was reaching its conclusion and he reached out to Christ for his acceptance and love, amazed and so thankful that he could be forgiven.

Within a day or two a letter from Alison arrived at Ian's mum with the news that they had both put their trust in Jesus Christ. Ian's father had died a short while earlier, still praying for his prodigal son.

Ian wrote 'Becoming a follower of Christ is the hardest thing I have ever done as it has changed everything – my behaviour, my values, my understanding and my thinking. But difficult as it has been I would choose no other way'.

Upon returning to the UK Ian and Alison were married and have had two other children. Life is not easy, the battles are not over, the memories remain. Alison writes: 'Life has continued to have many difficulties for us as a family, but we know that Jesus is with us through everything and we are so thankful for his love, forgiveness, patience, grace and mercy; for holding on to us when we haven't had the strength or faith to hold onto him. The Lord has changed our lives, but even more importantly and, amazingly, our eternities. All praise and thanks to God'.

If you haven't guessed already, I personally know Ian. He's my brother. I've witnessed this story firsthand. That's the power of the gospel. That's the hope we hold out. That's the life-transforming work of Jesus.

Jesus – do it again, many, many times over. And bring the prodigals home.

BIBLIOGRAPHY

Bartholomew, Craig and Goheen, Michael. *The Drama of Scripture*. SPCK, 2004.

Butterfield, Rosaria. *The Gospel Comes with a House Key*. Crossway, 2018.

Carswell, Roger. *And Some Evangelists*. Christian Focus, 2000.

Carswell, Roger. *Before You Say 'I Don't Believe'*. 10Publishing, 2014.

Chan, Sam. *Evangelism in a Skeptical World*. Zondervan, 2018.

Chapman, John. *Know and Tell the Gospel*. Hodder, 1981.

Chatraw, Joshua D. *Telling a Better Story*. Zondervan, 2020.

Chatraw, Joshua D. and Allen, Mark D. *Apologetics at the Cross*. Zondervan, 2018.

Chester, Tim. *Unreached: Growing Churches in Working-class and Deprived Areas*. IVP, 2012.

Coekin, Richard. *The Reluctant Evangelist*. The Good Book Company, 2018.

Craig, William Lane. *Hard Questions, Real Answers*. Crossway, 2003.

Dever, Mark. *The Gospel and Personal Evangelism*. Crossway, 2007.

Dickson, John. *Mission Commitment in Ancient Judaism and in the Pauline Communities*. Mohr Siebeck, 2003.

Dickson, John. *Promoting the Gospel*. Aquila Press, 2005.

Dickson, John. *The Best Kept Secret of Christian Mission*. Zondervan, 2010.

Goheen, Michael. *A Light to the Nations*. Baker Academic, 2011.

Goheen, Michael. *Introducing Christian Mission Today*. IVP Academic, 2014.

Goheen, Michael W. and Bartholomew, Craig G. *Living at the Crossroads*. Baker Books, 2008.

Gould, Paul M. *Cultural Apologetics*. Zondervan, 2019.

Harrison, Glynn. *A Better Story*. IVP, 2017.

Johnson, Dennis E. *Journeys with Jesus*. R&R, 2018.

Joslin, Roy. *Urban Harvest*. Evangelical Press, 1982.

Keller, Timothy. *Center Church Europe*. Zondervan, 2012.

Kreeft, Peter and Tacelli, Ronald K. *Handbook of Christian Apologetics*. IVP, 1994.

Lacey, Carolyn. *Extraordinary Hospitality (for Ordinary People)*. The Good Book Company, 2021.

Leonard, John S. *Get Real: Sharing Your Everyday faith Every Day*. New Growth Press, 2013.

Logan, Samuel T. (ed.). *Reformed Means Missional*. New Growth Press, 2013.

McConnell, Mez. *The Least, the Last and the Lost*. Evangelical Press, 2021.

McGrath, Alister E. *Narrative Apologetics*. Baker Books, 2019.

McLaughlin, Rebecca. *Confronting Christianity*. Crossway, 2019.

McLaughlin, Rebecca. *The Secular Creed*. The Gospel Coalition, 2021.

Newell, Marvin J. *Crossing Cultures in Scripture*. IVP, 2016.

Newman, Randy. *Mere Evangelism; 10 Insights from C. S. Lewis*. The Good Book Company, 2021.

Newman, Randy. *Questioning Evangelism*. Kregel, 2004.

Ots, Michael. *But Is It True?* IVP, 2016.

Ots, Michael. *Making Sense of Life*. 10Publishing, 2021.

Ots, Michael. *What Kind of Hope?* IVP, 2012.

Palmer, Bernard. *The Duty of a Disciple*. Christian Focus, 2020.

Pippert, Rebecca Manley. *Stay Salt*. The Good Book Company, 2020.

Platt, David. *Radical*. Multnomah, 2010.

Platt, David. *Radical Together*. Multnomah, 2011.

Richard, Randolph . and O'Brien, Brandon J. *Misreading Scripture with Western Eyes*. IVP, 2012.

Robertson, David. *Magnificent Obsession: Why Jesus is Great*. Christian Focus, 2013.

Scrivener, Glen. *321: The Story of God, the World and You*. 10Publishing, 2014.

Singlehurst, Laurence. *Sowing, Reaping Keeping: People-sensitive Evangelism*. IVP, 2006.

Stetzer, Ed and Im, Daniel. *Planting Missional Churches*. B&H, 2016.

Stiles, J. Mack. *Evangelism: How the Whole Church Speaks of Jesus*. Crossway, 2014.

Strange, Daniel. *Making Faith Magnetic*. The Good Book Company, 2021.

Strange, Daniel. *Plugged In*. The Good Book Company, 2019.

Stroope, Michael W. *Transcending Mission*. Apollos, 2017.

Tice, Rico. *Honest Evangelism*. The Good Book Company, 2015.

Trueman, Carl R. *The Rise and Triumph of the Modern Self*. Crossway, 2020.

Watson, David. *I believe in Evangelism*. Hodder, 1976.

Weston, Paul. *Why We can't Believe*. Frameworks, 1991.

Williams, Paul. *Intentional*. 10Publishing, 2016.

Willis, Dustin and Clements, Brandon. *The Simplest Way to Change the World: Biblical Hospitality as a Way of Life*. Moody, 2017.

Endnotes

1 B. Larson, P. Anderson and D. Self, *Mastering Pastoral Care. Mastering Ministry* series. (Multnomah Press / Christianity Today, 1990), p. 129.

2 NIV, 2011.

3 Colin Marshall and Tony Paine, *The Trellis and the Vine: The Ministry Mind-Shift That Changes Everything* (Matthias Media, 2009), p. 19.

4 Ibid. 49.

5 John Dickson, *Mission-Commitment in Ancient Judaism and in the Pauline Communities* (Mohr Siebeck, 2003), p. 131.

6 Dickson, *Mission-Commitment*, p. 143.

7 E.E. Ellis, *Paul and His Co-Workers.* New Testament Studies (Cambridge University Press, 1971), p. 15.

8 John Dickson, *Mission-Commitment*, p. 150.

9 Gordon P. Wiles, *Paul's Intercessory Prayers* (CUP, 2008), p. 296.

10 Robert J. Karris, *Eating Your Way through Luke's Gospel.* (Liturgical Press, 2006), p. 14.

11 Dave Kinnaman and Gabe Lyons, *unChristian: What A New Generation Really Thinks about Christianity. . . And Why It Matters* (Baker Books, 2012), p. 129.

12 John Dickson, *Mission-Commitment*, p. 277.

13 Adolf Harnack, *The Mission and Expansion of Christianity in the First Three Centuries* (Palala Press, 2015), vol. 1–31, pp. 367-8.

14 Carolyn Lacey, *Extraordinary Hospitality (for Ordinary People)* (The Good Book Company, 2021), p. 24.

15 Rosaria Butterfield, *The Gospel Comes with a House Key: Practicing Radically Ordinary Hospitality in Our Post-Christian World* (Crossway, 2018), p. 115.

16 Ibid, 85.

17 Ibid, 14.

18 Ibid, 51.

19 Jesvin Jose, Goodreads review of *Extraordinary Hospitality*.

20 C. Peter Wagner, *Church Planting for a Greater Harvest: A Comprehensive Guide* (Wipf & Stock, 2010), p. 11.

21 Wayne A. Grudem, *Systematic Theology: An Introduction to Biblical Doctrine* (Harper Collins, 2009), p. 624.

22 Whitefield's Letter to Wesley: Bethesda in Georgia, Dec. 24, 1740. Quoted by Robert F. Lay in *Readings in Historical Theology: Primary Sources of the Christian Faith* (Kregel Academic, 2009), p. 331.

23 John Stott, *The Message of 1 Timothy*. The Bible Speaks Today (IVP, 1996), p. 66.

24 Thomas Nagel, Logos: *A Journal of Catholic Thought and Culture* vol. 5, no. 2 (University of St. Thomas Spring, 2002), p. 160.

25 Anthony Curtis (ed.), John Whitehead (ed.). *W. Somerset Maugham: The Critical Heritage* (Routledge, 2013), p. 386.

26 Martin B. Copenhaver, *Jesus Is the Question: The 307 Questions Jesus Asked and the 3 He Answered* (Abingdon Press, 2014).

27 Randy Newman, *Questioning Evangelism*, 3rd ed. (Kregel Publications, 2023).

28 Paul Williams, *Intentional: Evangelism that Takes People to Jesus.* (10Publishing, 2016).

29 Daniel Strange, *Making Faith Magnetic: Five Hidden Themes Our Culture Can't Stop Talking about ... And How to Connect Them to Christ* (Surrey: The Good Book Company, 2021), p. 92.

30 Brooks Peterson, *Cultural Intelligence: A Guide to Working with People from Other Cultures*, 2nd ed. (Across Cultures, 2018).

31 Andy Crouch, 'The Return of Shame', *Christianity Today*, 10 March 2015.

32 'Suffering Opens a Door for the Gospel', desiringGod blog. 30 March 2017.

33 Ajith Fernando, *The Call to Joy and Pain: Embracing Suffering in Your Ministry* (Crossway Books, 2007), p. 83.

Christian Focus Publications

Our mission statement –

STAYING FAITHFUL

In dependence upon God we seek to impact the world through literature faithful to His infallible Word, the Bible. Our aim is to ensure that the Lord Jesus Christ is presented as the only hope to obtain forgiveness of sin, live a useful life and look forward to heaven with Him.

Our books are published in four imprints:

CHRISTIAN
FOCUS

Popular works including biographies, commentaries, basic doctrine and Christian living.

CHRISTIAN
HERITAGE

Books representing some of the best material from the rich heritage of the church.

MENTOR

Books written at a level suitable for Bible College and seminary students, pastors, and other serious readers. The imprint includes commentaries, doctrinal studies, examination of current issues and church history.

CF4•K

Children's books for quality Bible teaching and for all age groups: Sunday school curriculum, puzzle and activity books; personal and family devotional titles, biographies and inspirational stories – because you are never too young to know Jesus!

Christian Focus Publications Ltd,
Geanies House, Fearn, Ross-shire,
IV20 1TW, Scotland, United Kingdom.
www.christianfocus.com